KNIFE FIGHTING

TARGETS

THE ULTIMATE KNIFE FIGHTING TARGETING SYSTEM FOR SELF-DEFENSE

SAMMY FRANCO

Also by Sammy Franco

Knife Fighting: A Step-by-Step Guide to Practical Knife Fighting for Self-Defense
Cane Fighting
The Heavy Bag Bible
The Widow Maker Compendium
Invincible: Mental Toughness Techniques for Peak Performance
Unleash Hell: A Step-by-Step Guide to Devastating Widow Maker Combinations
Feral Fighting: Advanced Widow Maker Fighting Techniques
The Widow Maker Program: Extreme Self-Defense for Deadly Force Situations
Savage Street Fighting: Tactical Savagery as a Last Resort
Heavy Bag Workout
Heavy Bag Combinations
Heavy Bag Training
The Complete Body Opponent Bag Book
Stand and Deliver: A Street Warrior's Guide to Tactical Combat Stances
Maximum Damage: Hidden Secrets Behind Brutal Fighting Combinations
First Strike: End a Fight in Ten Seconds or Less!
The Bigger They Are, The Harder They Fall
Self-Defense Tips and Tricks
Kubotan Power: Quick & Simple Steps to Mastering the Kubotan Keychain
Gun Safety: For Home Defense and Concealed Carry
Out of the Cage: A Guide to Beating a Mixed Martial Artist on the Street
Warrior Wisdom: Inspiring Ideas from the World's Greatest Warriors
War Machine: How to Transform Yourself Into a Vicious and Deadly Street Fighter
1001 Street Fighting Secrets
When Seconds Count: Self-Defense for the Real World
Killer Instinct: Unarmed Combat for Street Survival
Street Lethal: Unarmed Urban Combat

Knife Fighting Targets: The Ultimate Knife Fighting Targeting System for Self-Defense
Copyright © 2018 by Sammy Franco
ISBN: 978-1-941845-64-6
Printed in the United States of America

Published by Contemporary Fighting Arts, LLC.
Visit us Online at: **ContemporaryFightingArts.com**

For author interviews or publicity information, please send inquiries in care of the publisher.

Contents

"The worst-case scenario of a knife fight is you die, and the best-case scenario is you go to prison."

– Anonymous

Warning!

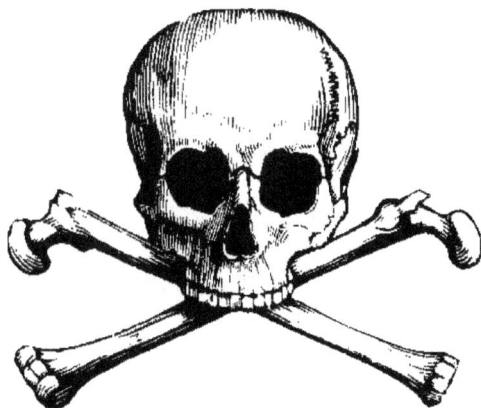

The intent of this book is to provide general information about knife fighting techniques for personal self-defense and to help define areas of knife training that the reader may choose to further investigate. This program is for academic study only.

Moreover, the author, publisher and distributor do not intend for any of the information contained in this book to be used for criminal purposes. This book is about an art form and should be viewed as such.

The techniques, tactics, methods, and information described and depicted in this book can be dangerous and could result in serious injury and or death and should not be used or practiced in any way without the guidance of a qualified self-defense instructor.

The following is meant to supplement a safe edged weapon-training program. Never practice knife training without the supervision of a qualified knife-fighting instructor. Never, ever practice with sharpened or live blades. This book is for information purposes only. Please consult with local laws in your area concerning the practice of martial arts, knife sparring, and ownership or carrying of simulated weapons.

Knife fighting training is dangerous. The author, publisher, and distributors of this manual will accept no responsibility, nor are they liable to any person or entity whatsoever for any injury, damage, or loss of any sort that may arise out of practicing, teaching, or disseminating of any techniques or ideas contained herein. You assume full responsibility for the use of the information in this program and agree that the author, distributor and contributors hold no liability to you for claims, damages, costs and expenses, legal fees, or any other costs incurred due to or in any way related to your reliance on anything derived from this program or its contents.

Additionally, it is the reader's responsibility to research and comply with all local, state, and federal laws and regulations pertaining to the possession, carry, and use of edged weapons. This program is for educational reference information only!

The use of a knife or edged weapons denotes the use of deadly force and is subject to the laws of each state or local jurisdiction. Readers must assume all liability for their subsequent actions and edged weapon practices. The author, publisher, distributor and all product providers assume no liability for any actions made by readers of this program.

Before you begin any exercise program, including those suggested in this manual, it is important to check with your physician to see if you have any condition that might be aggravated by strenuous exercise.

About Knife Fighting Targets

Knife Fighting Targets: The Ultimate Knife Fighting Targeting System for Self-Defense is a concise book designed to teach you the most practical and effective knife fighting targets for real-world self-defense.

The knife fighting targets featured in this book apply to both fixed blades as well as fighting folders and can be readily used by young and old, regardless of size or strength. Most importantly, you don't need martial arts training to understand and ultimately master these effective knife fighting targets.

Unlike other knife fighting books, Knife Fighting Targets is devoid of complicated, impractical and gimmicky techniques that can get you injured or possibly killed during a deadly knife fight. Instead, this book arms you with efficient, effective, and practical knife fighting skills that work in the chaos of life and death edged weapon encounter.

Practitioners who regularly practice the knife targeting featured in this book will establish a rock solid foundation for using a knife for self-defense. Moreover, the techniques featured in this book will significantly improve your overall personal protection skills, enhance your conditioning, and introduce you to a new method of personal protection.

This book is based on my 30+ years of research, training and teaching reality-based self-defense and combat sciences. I've taught

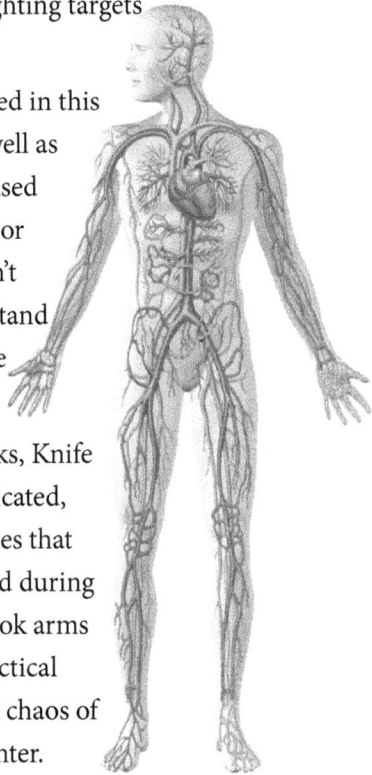

these unique knife fighting skills to thousands of my students, and I'm confident they can help protect you and your loved ones during an emergency situation.

The information, techniques, and suggestions contained herein are dangerous and should only be used to protect yourself or a loved one from the immediate risk of unlawful injury. Remember, the decision to use a knife for self-defense must always be a last resort, after all other means of avoiding violence have been thoroughly exhausted.

Finally, Knife Fighting Targets is based on my best selling book, Knife Fighting: A Step-By-Step Guide to Practical Knife Fighting for Self-Defense. Therefore, if you desire a more in-depth study of the art of knife combat, I suggest picking up a copy.

Be safe!

Sammy Franco
ContemporaryFightingArts.com

Introduction
Contemporary Fighting Arts

Knife Fighting Targets

Exploring Contemporary Fighting Arts

Before diving head first into this book, I'd like to first introduce you to my unique system of fighting, Contemporary Fighting Arts (CFA). I hope it will give you a greater understanding and appreciation of the material covered in this book. And for those of you who are already familiar with CFA, you can skip to the next chapter.

Contemporary Fighting Arts® (CFA), is a state-of-the-art combat system that was introduced to the world in 1983. This sophisticated and practical system of self-defense is designed specifically to provide efficient and effective methods to avoid, defuse, confront, and neutralize both armed and unarmed assailants in a variety of deadly situations and circumstances.

Unlike karate, kung-fu, mixed martial arts and the like, CFA is the first offensive-based American martial art that is specifically designed for the violence that plagues our cruel city streets. CFA dispenses with the extraneous and the impractical and focuses on real-life street fighting.

Every tool, technique and tactic found within the CFA system must meet three essential criteria for fighting: efficiency, effectiveness, and safety. Efficiency means that the techniques permit you to reach your combative objective quickly and economically. Effectiveness means that the elements of the system will produce the desired effect. Finally, Safety means that the combative elements provide the least amount of danger and risk for you - the fighter.

CFA is not about mind-numbing tournaments or senseless competition. It does not require you to waste time and energy practicing forms (katas) or other impractical rituals. There are no theatrical kicks or exotic techniques. Finally, CFA does not adhere blindly to tradition for tradition's sake. Simply put, it is a scientific yet pragmatic approach to staying alive on the streets.

CFA has been taught to people of all walks of life. Some include the U.S. Border Patrol, police officers, deputy sheriffs, security guards, military personnel, private investigators, surgeons, lawyers, college professors, airline pilots, as well as black belts, boxers, and kick boxers. CFA's broad appeal results from its ability to teach people how to really fight.

It's All In The Name!

Before discussing the three components that make up Contemporary Fighting Arts, it is important to understand how CFA acquired its unique name. To begin, the first word, "Contemporary," was selected because it refers to the system's modern, up-to-date orientation. Unlike traditional martial arts, CFA is specifically designed to meet the challenges of our modern world.

The second term, "Fighting," was chosen because it accurately describes the system's combat orientation. After all, why not just call it Contemporary Martial Arts? There are two reasons for this. First, the word "martial" conjures up images of traditional and impractical martial art forms that are antithetical to the system. Second, why dilute a perfectly functional name when the word "fighting" defines the system so succinctly? Contemporary Fighting Arts is about teaching people how to really fight.

Let's look at the last word, "Arts." In the subjective sense, "art" refers to the combat skills that are acquired through arduous study, practice, and observation. The bottom line is that effective street fighting skills will require consistent practice and attention. Take, for example, something as seemingly basic as an elbow strike, which will actually require hundreds of hours of practice to perfect.

The pluralization of the word "Art" reflects CFA's protean instruction. The various components of CFA's training (i.e., firearms training, stick fighting, ground fighting, natural body weapon mastery, and so on) have all truly earned their status as individual art forms and, as such, require years of consistent study and practice to perfect. To acquire a greater understanding of CFA, here is an overview of the system's three vital components: the physical, the mental, and the spiritual.

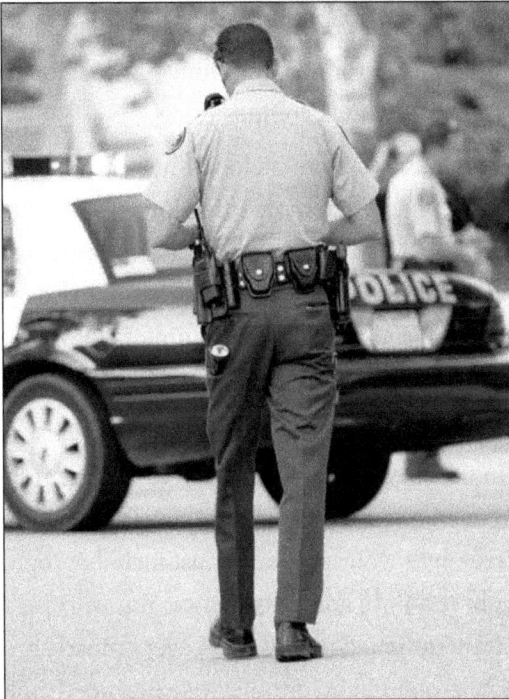

Police officers need practical and effective defensive tactics for dealing with violent street criminals. This is why many law enforcement officers seek out Contemporary Fighting Arts training.

The Physical Component

The physical component of CFA focuses on the physical development of a fighter, including physical fitness, weapon and technique mastery, and self-defense attributes.

Physical Fitness

If you are going to prevail in a street fight, you must be physically fit. It's that simple. In fact, you will never master the tools and skills of combat unless you're in excellent physical shape. On the average, you will have to spend more than an hour a day to achieve maximum fitness.

In CFA physical fitness comprises the following three broad components: cardiorespiratory conditioning, muscular/skeletal conditioning, and proper body composition.

The cardiorespiratory system includes the heart, lungs, and circulatory system, which undergo tremendous stress during the course of a street fight. So you're going to have to run, jog, bike, swim, or skip rope to develop sound cardiorespiratory conditioning. Each aerobic workout should last a minimum of 30 minutes and be performed at least four times per week.

The second component of physical fitness is muscular/skeletal conditioning. In the streets, the strong survive and the rest go to the morgue. To strengthen your bones and muscles to withstand the rigors of a real fight, your program must include progressive resistance (weight training) and calisthenics. You will also need a stretching program designed to loosen up every muscle group. You can't kick, punch, ground fight, or otherwise execute the necessary body mechanics if you're "tight" or inflexible. Stretching on a regular basis will also increase the muscles' range of motion, improve circulation, reduce the possibility of injury, and relieve daily stress.

The final component of physical fitness is proper body composition: simply, the ratio of fat to lean body tissue. Your diet and training regimen will affect your level or percentage of body fat significantly. A sensible and consistent exercise program accompanied by a healthy and balanced diet will facilitate proper body composition. Do not neglect this important aspect of physical fitness.

Weapon and Technique Mastery

You won't stand a chance against a vicious assailant if you don't master the weapons and tools of fighting. In CFA, we teach our students both armed and unarmed methods of combat. Unarmed fighting requires that you master a complete arsenal of natural body weapons and techniques. In conjunction, you must also learn the various stances, hand positioning, footwork, body mechanics, defensive structure, locks, chokes, and various holds. Keep in mind that something as simple as a basic punch will actually require hundreds of hours to perfect.

Range proficiency is another important aspect of weapon and technique mastery. Briefly, range proficiency is the ability to fight effectively in all three ranges of unarmed fighting. Although punching range tools are emphasized in CFA, kicking and grappling ranges cannot be neglected. Our kicking range tools consist of deceptive and powerful low-line kicks. Grappling range tools include head-butts, elbows, knees, foot stomps, biting, tearing, gouging, and crushing tactics.

Although CFA focuses on striking, we also teach our students a myriad of chokes, locks, and holds that can be used in a ground fight. While such grappling range submission techniques are not the most preferred methods of dealing with a ground fighting situation, they must be studied for the following six reasons: (1) level of force - many ground fighting situations do not justify the use of deadly force. In such instances, you must apply various non-lethal submission holds, (2) nature of the beast - in order to escape any choke, lock or hold, you must first know how to apply them yourself, (3) occupational

Knife Fighting Targets

requirement- some professional occupations (police, security, etc.) require that you possess a working knowledge of various submission techniques, (4) subduing a friend or relative - in many cases it is best to restrain and control a friend or relative with a submission hold instead of striking him with a natural body weapon, (5) anatomical orientation - practicing various chokes, locks and holds will help you develop a strong orientation of the human anatomy, and (6) refutation requirement - finally, if you are going to criticize the combative limitations of any submission hold, you better be sure that you can perform it yourself.

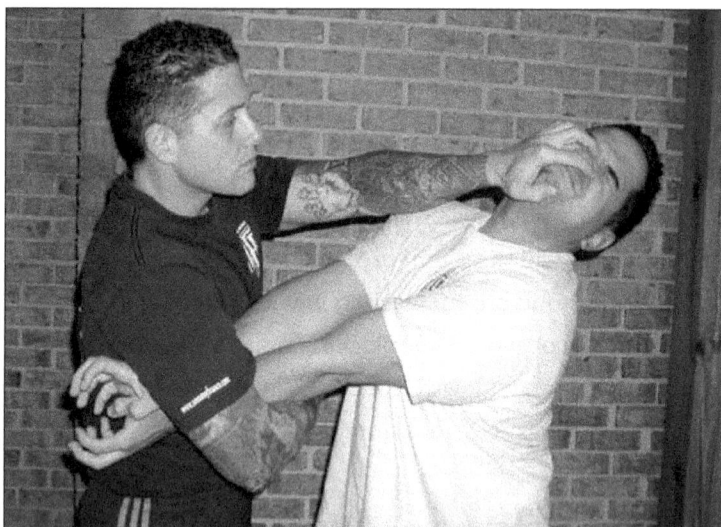

Contemporary Fighting Arts is more than a self defense system, its a one-of-a-kind martial arts style geared for real world self defense.

Defensive tools and skills are also taught. Our defensive structure is efficient, uncomplicated, and impenetrable. It provides the fighter maximum protection while allowing complete freedom of choice for acquiring offensive control. Our defensive structure is based on distance, parrying, blocking, evading, mobility, and stance structure.

Simplicity is always the key.

Students are also instructed in specific methods of armed fighting. For example, CFA provides instruction about firearms for personal and household protection. We provide specific guidelines for handgun purchasing, operation, nomenclature, proper caliber, shooting fundamentals, cleaning, and safe storage. Our firearm program also focuses on owner responsibility and the legal ramifications regarding the use of deadly force.

CFA's weapons program also consists of natural body weapons, knives and edged weapons, single and double stick, makeshift weaponry, the side-handle baton, and oleoresin capsicum (OC) spray.

Combat Attributes

Your offensive and defensive tools are useless unless they are used strategically. For any tool or technique to be effective in a real fight, it must be accompanied by specific attributes. Attributes are qualities that enhance a particular tool, technique, or maneuver. Some examples include speed, power, timing, coordination, accuracy, non-telegraphic movement, balance, and target orientation.

CFA also has a wide variety of training drills and methodologies designed to develop and sharpen these combat attributes. For example, our students learn to ground fight while blindfolded, spar with one arm tied down, and fight while handcuffed.

Reality is the key. For example, in class students participate in full-contact exercises against fully padded assailants, and real weapon disarms are rehearsed and analyzed in a variety of dangerous scenarios. Students also train with a large variety of equipment, including heavy bags, double-end bags, uppercut bags, pummel bags, focus mitts, striking shields, mirrors, rattan sticks, foam and plastic bats, kicking pads, knife drones, trigger-sensitive (mock) guns, boxing and digit gloves, full-body armor, and hundreds of different environmental props.

There are more than two hundred unique training methodologies used in Contemporary Fighting Arts. Each one is scientifically designed to prepare students for the hard-core realities of real world combat. There are also three specific training methodologies used to develop and sharpen the fundamental attributes and skills of armed and unarmed fighting, including proficiency training, conditioning training, and street training.

CFA has a several unique military combat training programs. Our mission is to provide today's modern soldier with the knowledge, skills and attitude necessary to survive a wide variety of real world combat scenarios. Our military program is designed to provide the modern soldier with the safest and most effective skills and tactics to control and decentralize armed and unarmed enemies.

Proficiency training can be used for both armed and unarmed skills. When conducted properly, proficiency training develops speed, power, accuracy, non-telegraphic movement, balance, and general psychomotor skill. The training objective is to sharpen one specific body weapon, maneuver, or technique at a time by executing

Introduction

it over and over for a prescribed number of repetitions. Each time
the technique or maneuver is executed with "clean" form at various
speeds. Movements are also performed with the eyes closed to
develop a kinesthetic "feel" for the action. Proficiency training can
be accomplished through the use of various types of equipment,
including the heavy bag, double-end bag, focus mitts, training knives,
real and mock pistols, striking shields, shin and knee guards, foam
and plastic bats, mannequin heads, and so on.

Conditioning training develops endurance, fluidity, rhythm,
distancing, timing, speed, footwork, and balance. In most cases,
this type of training requires the student to deliver a variety of
fighting combinations for three- or four-minute rounds separated by
30-second breaks. Like proficiency training, this type of training can
also be performed at various speeds. A good workout consists of at
least five rounds. Conditioning training can be performed on the bags
with full-contact sparring gear, rubber training knives, focus mitts,
kicking shields, and shin guards, or against imaginary assailants in
shadow fighting.

Conditioning training is not necessarily limited to just three- or
four-minute rounds. For example, CFA's ground fighting training can
last as long as 30 minutes. The bottom line is that it all depends on
what you are training for.

Street training is the final preparation for the real thing. Since
many violent altercations are explosive, lasting an average of 20
seconds, you must prepare for this possible scenario. This means
delivering explosive and powerful compound attacks with vicious
intent for approximately 20 seconds, resting one minute, and then
repeating the process.

Street training prepares you for the stress and immediate fatigue
of a real fight. It also develops speed, power, explosiveness, target
selection and recognition, timing, footwork, pacing, and breath

control. You should practice this methodology in different lighting, on different terrains, and in different environmental settings. You can use different types of training equipment as well. For example, you can prepare yourself for multiple assailants by having your training partners attack you with focus mitts from a variety of angles, ranges, and target postures. For 20 seconds, go after them with vicious low-line kicks, powerful punches, and devastating strikes.

When all is said and done, the physical component creates a fighter who is physically fit and armed with a lethal arsenal of tools, techniques, and weapons that can be deployed with destructive results.

The Mental Component

The mental component of CFA focuses on the cerebral aspects of a fighter, developing killer instinct, strategic/tactical awareness, analysis and integration skills, philosophy, and cognitive skills.

The Killer Instinct

Deep within each of us is a cold and deadly primal power known as the "killer instinct." The killer instinct is a vicious combat mentality that surges to your consciousness and turns you into a fierce fighter who is free of fear, anger, and apprehension. If you want to survive the horrifying dynamics of real criminal violence, you must cultivate and utilize this instinctive killer mentality.

There are 14 characteristics of CFA's killer instinct. They are: (1) clear and lucid thinking, (2) heightened situational awareness, (3) adrenaline surge, (4) mobilized body, (5) psychomotor control, (6) absence of distraction, (7) tunnel vision, (8) fearless mind-set, (9) tactical implementation, (10) the lack of emotion, (11) breath control, (12) pseudospeciation, (13) viciousness, and (14) pain tolerance.

Visualization and crisis rehearsal are just two techniques used to develop, refine, and channel this extraordinary source of strength and energy so that it can be used to its full potential.

Strategic/Tactical Awareness

Strategy is the bedrock of preparedness. In CFA, there are three unique categories of strategic awareness that will diminish the likelihood of criminal victimization. They are criminal awareness, situational awareness, and self-awareness. When developed, these essential skills prepare you to assess a wide variety of threats instantaneously and accurately. Once you've made a proper threat assessment, you will be able to choose one of the following five self-defense options: comply, escape, de-escalate, assert, or fight back.

CFA also teaches students to assess a variety of other important factors, including the assailant's demeanor, intent, range, positioning and weapon capability, as well as such environmental issues as escape routes, barriers, terrain, and makeshift weaponry. In addition to assessment skills, CFA also teaches students how to enhance perception and observation skills.

Analysis and Integration Skills

The analytical process is intricately linked to understanding how to defend yourself in any threatening situation. If you want to be the best, every aspect of fighting and personal protection must be dissected. Every strategy, tactic, movement, and concept must be broken down to its atomic parts. The three planes (physical, mental, spiritual) of self-defense must be unified scientifically through arduous practice and constant exploration.

CFA's most advanced practitioners have sound insight and understanding of a wide range of sciences and disciplines. They include human anatomy, kinesiology, criminal justice, sociology, kinesics, proxemics, combat physics, emergency medicine, crisis management, histrionics, police and military science, the psychology of aggression, and the role of archetypes.

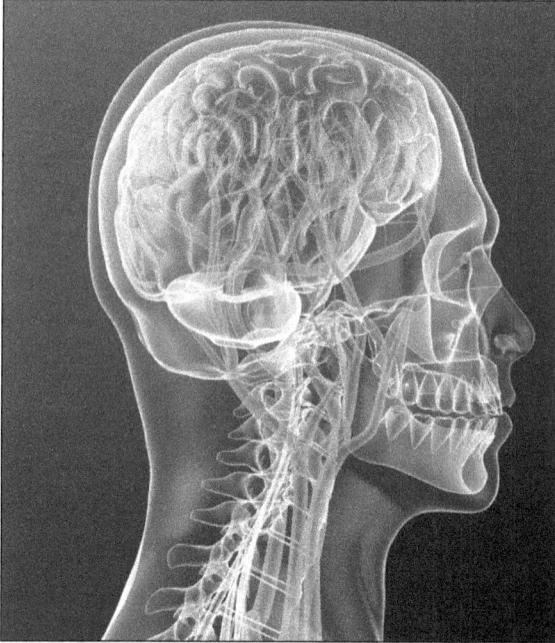

CFA's mental component focuses on the cognitive development of a fighter, including strategic/tactical awareness, analysis and integration, cognitive skills, the killer instinct, and philosophy.

Analytical exercises are also a regular part of CFA training. For example, we conduct problem-solving sessions involving particular assailants attacking in defined environments. We move hypothetical attackers through various ranges to provide insight into tactical solutions. We scrutinize different methods of attack for their general utility in combat. We also discuss the legal ramifications of self-defense on a frequent basis.

In addition to problem-solving sessions, students are slowly exposed to concepts of integration and modification. Oral and written examinations are given to measure intellectual accomplishment. Unlike traditional systems, CFA does not use colored belts or sashes to identify the student's level of proficiency.

Philosophy

Philosophical resolution is essential to a fighter's mental confidence and clarity. Anyone learning the art of war must find the ultimate answers to questions concerning the use of violence in defense of himself or others. To advance to the highest levels of combat awareness, you must find clear and lucid answers to such provocative questions as could you take the life of another, what are your fears, who are you, why are you interested in studying Contemporary Fighting Arts, why are you reading this book, and what is good and what is evil? If you haven't begun the quest to

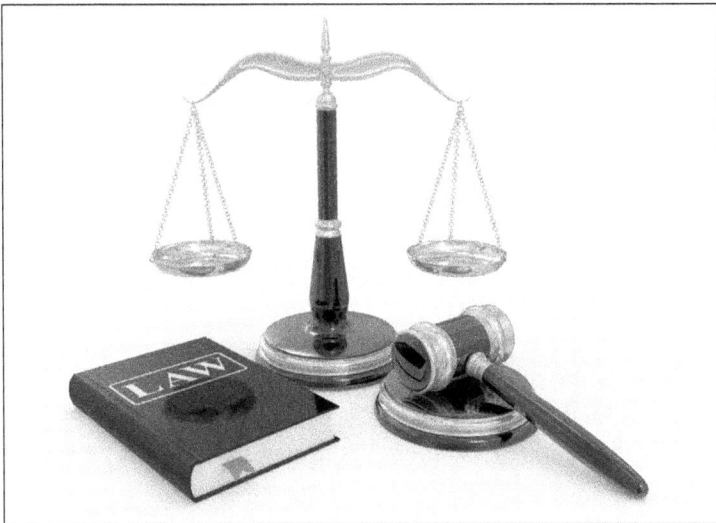

Developing a deadly capability to protect yourself carries tremendous moral and social responsibility. It also involves the risk of civil liability and criminal jeopardy. There is an interesting irony facing most martial artists or self-defense experts. The more highly trained, knowledgeable, and skilled you are in firearms, knives, unarmed combat tactics, martial arts, and other self-defense skills, the higher the standards of care you must follow when protecting yourself and others.

formulate these important questions and answers, then take a break. It's time to figure out just why you want to know the laws and rules of destruction.

Cognitive Combat Skills

Cognitive combat exercises are also important for improving one's fighting skills. CFA uses visualization and crisis rehearsal scenarios to improve general body mechanics, tools and techniques, and maneuvers, as well as tactic selection. Mental clarity, concentration, and emotional control are also developed to enhance one's ability to call upon the controlled killer instinct.

The Spiritual Component

There are many tough fighters out there. In fact, they reside in every town in every country. However, most are nothing more than vicious animals that lack self-mastery. And self-mastery is what separates the true warrior from the eternal novice.

I am not referring to religious precepts or beliefs when I speak of CFA's spiritual component. Unlike most martial arts, CFA does not merge religion into its spiritual aspect. Religion is a very personal and private matter and should never, be incorporated into any fighting system.

CFA's spiritual component is not something that is taught or studied. Rather, it is that which transcends the physical and mental aspects of being and reality. There is a deeper part of each of us that is a tremendous source of truth and accomplishment.

In CFA, the spiritual component is something that is slowly and progressively acquired. During the challenging quest of combat training, one begins to tap the higher qualities of human nature. Those elements of our being that inherently enable us to know right from wrong and good from evil. As we slowly develop this aspect of our total self, we begin to strengthen qualities profoundly important to the "truth." Such qualities are essential to your growth through the mastery of inner peace, the clarity of your "vision," and your recognition of universal truths.

While there are many dedicated individuals who are more than qualified to teach unique philosophical and spiritual components of ancient martial arts, you must realize that such forms of combat can get you killed in a real life self-defense encounter.

One of the goals of my system is to promote virtue and moral responsibility in people who have extreme capacities for physical and mental destructiveness. The spiritual component of fighting is truly the most difficult aspect of personal growth. Yet, unlike the physical component, where the practitioner's abilities will be limited to some degree by genetics and other natural factors, the spiritual component of combat offers unlimited potential for growth and development. In the final analysis, CFA's spiritual component poses the greatest challenges for the student. It is an open-ended plane of unlimited advancement.

Knife Fighting Targets

Chapter 1
Avoiding A Knife Fight

Knife Fighting Targets

Four Knife Survival Concepts

Before jumping into specific knife fighting targets, it's important first to cover a few important concepts that will significantly enhance your safety and survival prior to and during a knife fight. They include the following:

- **Situational Awareness**
- **Threat Assessment**
- **Avoiding Excessive Force**
- **Controlling Fear**

Situational Awareness

Situational awareness is total alertness, presence, and focus on virtually everything in your immediate surroundings. You must train your senses to detect and assess the people, places, objects, and actions that can pose a danger to you. Do not think of situational awareness simply in terms of the five customary senses of sight, sound, smell, taste, and touch. In addition, the very real powers of instinct and intuition must also be developed and eventually relied upon.

Two vagrants congregating on the street corner or by your car, the stranger lingering at the mailboxes in your lobby, the delivery man at the door, a deserted parking lot, an alleyway near a familiar sidewalk, the stray dog ambling toward you in the park, a large limb hanging precariously from a tree . . . these are all obvious examples of persons, places, and objects that can pose a threat to you. Situational awareness need not - and should not - be limited to preconceived notions about obvious sources of danger.

Unfortunately, very few people have refined their situational awareness skills. The reasons are many. Some are in denial about the prevalence of criminal violence while others are too distracted

Knife Fighting Targets

by life's everyday problems and pressures to pay attention to the hidden dangers that lurk around them. Whatever the reasons, poor awareness skills can get you into serious trouble and could cost you your life.

During a SHTF situation, situational awareness is total alertness, presence, and focus on virtually everything in your immediate surroundings.

Situational awareness, in terms of threats posed by a knife wielding adversary, begins with an understanding of criminal psychology. It is a common misconception that criminals are stupid and incompetent. Although many may be uneducated by traditional standards, they are not stupid. On the contrary, they can be shrewd, methodical, bold, and psychologically dominant. The especially dangerous ones are often expert observers of human behavior, capable of accurately assessing your body language, walk, talk, carriage, state of mind, and a variety of other indicators. They know what to look for and how to exploit it.

Chapter 1: Avoiding A Knife Fight

Criminals are also selective predators. Many rapists, for example, will test a victim by engaging her in idle conversation, following her, or invading her space in some preliminary and seemingly harmless manner. Carefully selected measures designed to evaluate fear, apprehension, and awareness are part of the attacker's overall strategy. Seasoned criminal aggressors are looking for easy strikes - what they call the "vic." Chronic brawlers, street punks, and muggers operate in the same basic manner. They look for the weak, timid, disoriented, and unaware victims.

As you develop situational awareness, you transmit a different kind of signal to the enemy's radar. Weakness and uncertainty are replaced by confidence and strength. Your carriage and movements change. You will be seen as assertive and purposeful. You are less likely to be perceived as an easy mark or a "vic," and your chances of being attacked will significantly diminish.

Situational awareness also diminishes the potency of the criminal's favorite weapon—surprise. Your ability to foresee and detect danger will diminish his ability to stalk you, or lie in wait in ambush zones. Ambush zones are strategic locations from which criminal assailants launch their attacks. Every day millions of Americans walk through numerous ambush zones and never even know it. Ambush zones are everywhere. They can be found and exploited in unfamiliar and familiar environments, even in your home, and in unpopulated and populated areas. An ambush zone can be set in a dark or poorly lit area as well as in a well-lit area. An ambush zone can be established in a variety of common places: under, behind, or around trees, utility boxes, shrubs, beds, corners, dumpsters, doorways, walls, tables, cars, trash cans, rooftops, bridges, ramps, mailboxes, etc. They are everywhere!

In addition to enhancing your ability to detect, avoid, and strategically neutralize ambush zones, situational awareness

Knife Fighting Targets

allows you to detect and avoid threats and dangers not necessarily predicated on the element of surprise. Some situations afford potential victims the luxury of actually seeing trouble coming. Nonetheless, it's remarkable how many people fail to heed obvious signs of danger because of poor awareness skills. They overlook the signals—belligerence, furtiveness, hostility, restlessness—so often manifested by criminal attackers. They neglect the opportunity to cross the street long before the shoulder-to-shoulder encounter with a pack of young toughs moving up the sidewalk. Once it's too late to avoid the confrontation, a whole new range of principles comes

Ambush zones are everywhere, how many do you see in this photo?

quickly into play. The best defense is a heightened level of situational awareness. You must learn to avoid situations that will require the use of your knife, and the highest form of self-defense is being smart enough to avoid a knife fight in the first place.

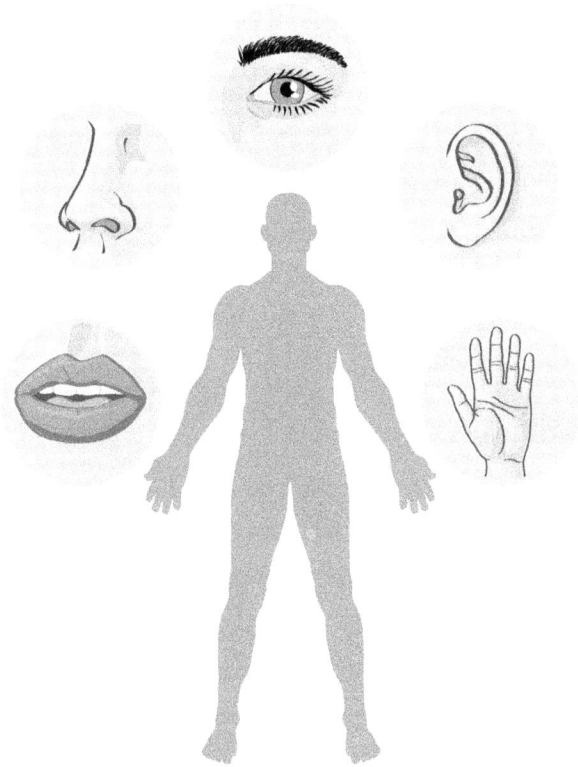

Situational awareness requires you to train all of your senses to detect and assess the people, places, objects, and actions that can pose a danger to you and your loved ones.

Situational Awareness Exercises

1. Detect five different ambush zones at your workplace and write them down. Don't pick the obvious ones. It's your life; learn to think like the criminal.

2. Detect five different ambush zones in front of your home. If you didn't find five, you didn't look hard enough.

3. Over the next ten days do not allow yourself to be taken by surprise—by anyone! Every time it happens, record the circumstances: who, what, when, how, where, and why.

4. When you watch television, go to the movies, look at pictures, or read books, note ambush zones that have not occurred to you in your other assessments. Note them in writing.

5. Visualize five different settings. They can be friendly and familiar like your backyard, or hostile and strange. Write down the things that you have mentally noted in these visualized settings.

Self Awareness

Self-awareness has been the subject of philosophers and mystics for centuries. Socrates said, "Know thyself." He believed self-knowledge to be essential to the attainment of true virtue.

Self-awareness is a critical component of knife fighting, but what does it mean to know yourself? Of course, you know your tastes and preferences, your desires, your occupation, and so forth. But do you know who you really are? What aspects of your self provoke violence and which, if any, would promote a proper reaction in defense against a threat of violence to you or others? Let's look at certain aspects important to knife fighting and ask ourselves a few tough questions.

Physical Attributes

What are your physical strengths and weaknesses? Are you overweight or underweight? Is your body language and the manner in which you carry yourself more likely to provoke or deter a violent attack? Do you have any training in knife fighting? Are you fit or out of shape? Do you have the skill to disarm a knife-wielding attacker? Do you smoke or drink excessively?

Mental Attributes

What are your mental strengths and weaknesses? Are you an optimist or pessimist? Can you summon up courage and confidence even when you are feeling fearful or insecure? How do you handle stress? Do you panic or frighten easily? Do you have any phobias? What are your fears? Do you think well on your feet?

Communication Skills

What are your strengths and weaknesses in expressing yourself with words? Are you likely to aggravate or diffuse a hostile situation? Are your words congruent with your tone of voice? Can you communicate adequately under stressful situations, or do you become nonplused?

Personality Traits

What type of person are you? Are you passive or aggressive? Are you opinionated and argumentative or open-minded and deliberative? Are you fiery, loud, and boisterous, or quiet, subdued, and calm? Are you quick to anger? Do you harbor grudges? Are there sensitive issues or remarks that may cause you to lose your temper?

Gender and Age

What are the different types of violent crimes that are directed toward you because of your sex? Women are much more likely than men to be raped or abused by their spouses. On the other hand, males are more apt than females to be victims of homicides. Is your age an open invitation for an attack? Children are more likely to be molested or kidnapped than adults, and older adults are weaker and more vulnerable to attack than middle-aged people.

Knife Fighting Targets

Occupation

Does the nature of your occupation make you or your family vulnerable to different forms of criminal violence? Are you involved with the military or law enforcement? Are you a celebrity? Do you have diplomatic or political connections? Do you control large sums of money or valuable drugs? Does your political affiliation make you or your family a likely target for kidnapping and terrorism?

Income Level

What types of crime are directed toward you because of your income level? Are you wealthy, comfortable, or poor? Does your income level make you and your family vulnerable to kidnapping for ransom? Or does your financial situation force you and your family to live in poor neighborhoods that invite violent crime? Are you wealthy and flashy with outward evidence of this wealth?

Self-Awareness Exercises

The following questions were designed to start you thinking in the important process of self-awareness. Use them to form an overall personal profile of yourself. The goal is to recognize traits that provoke and/or prevent a possible knife fight.

1. Think of five physical and five mental weaknesses that would inhibit your survival in a knife fighting situation.

2. Recall a very stressful situation. How did you react? How did you feel? Were you angry? Did you lose control? Were you calm, notwithstanding the pressure?

3. Ask a close friend or your spouse to evaluate your communication skills in a variety of situations with other people. Are you open and receptive, rude or polite, emphatic and expressive, or reserved and withdrawn? Do not react defensively to the critique you receive, even if you don't agree.

4. Look into the mirror and conjure up the following mental and emotional states, carefully noting your facial expressions as they arise: anger, happiness, sadness, depression, surprise, and fear.

5. Go back to the preceding exercise and focus on anger. Pay close attention to your facial expressions and other physiological manifestations. What do you see?

6. Think of three forms of violent crime that you may be subject to because of your lifestyle.

7. Think of three forms of violent crime that you may be subject to because of your gender.

8. To gain a better understanding of yourself, complete the following four exercises. Be frank and truthful.

-   Do you believe you could take the life of another human being if you had to?

-   List four of your greatest fears.

-   What steps might you take to eliminate or diminish those fears?

-   Name three issues, topics, comments, or situations that would provoke you to lose your temper.

What is Threat Assessment?

We assess many different things every day. For example, we assess such divergent things as shopping values, the pros and cons of career moves, and different aspects of our relationships with others. The requisite skills for these assessments vary, depending on the elements involved. Skills for assessing the effect of fluctuating interest rates on the stock market are very different from those necessary to assess the effect of a volcano on global weather patterns. The analytical processes may be similar, but the knowledge and skills need to be encountered individually, and not arbitrarily.

Similarly, in the world of knife combat, threat assessment is the process of rapidly gathering and analyzing information, then accurately evaluating it in terms of threat and danger. In general, you can assess people, places, objects, and actions. In addition, assessment skills require sharp perception and keen observation. Your perception skills can be heightened, and your ability to observe can be enhanced.

Threat assessment is the process of rapidly gathering and analyzing information, then accurately evaluating it in terms of threat and danger.

We gather information through our sensory processes. You see a movement in the shadows of your backyard. You hear footsteps approaching from behind you in a dark parking lot. You smell cigarette smoke in what you thought was a deserted area. You feel a breeze coming up your stairwell when all the doors and windows are supposed to be shut. You taste the sickening metallic flavor of fear in your mouth.

These five senses can be sharpened through a variety of exercises designed to develop both raw detection and learned identification capabilities. For example, sit alone in your backyard for a given period of time and catalog the various things your five senses detect. Next, list the possible sources of the sensory data. With practice, you will make remarkable progress from being unable to detect a particular sound or smell to not only detecting it quickly and accurately but also identifying its source. This development increases as these exercises are performed in different types of settings. Imagine, for example, the things you would hear, see, and smell on a dark night in the middle of a suburban park, as opposed to what you would experience standing in a dark urban alley. Remember, you are only limited by your imagination.

Additionally, you can also heighten your ability to observe. Have you ever noticed how keenly you study people, buildings, streets, signs, animals, and various other everyday things when you travel to a strange city or to another country? Watch a dog in a new environment, with its nose in the air and ears perked in alertness. People and animals tend to observe more actively in strange or new environments. This practice reveals an old survival process at work. Conversely, we tend to become less observant in familiar settings. We let our guard down, so to speak. For example, how many times has your wife or girlfriend changed her hair, or your husband or boyfriend shaved his beard, and you simply didn't notice it?

Here's the good news: observational skills can be expanded with application of an intelligent program. In my Contemporary Fighting Arts (CFA) self-defense system, students are instructed to practice quickly, memorizing lines of verse in a hectic setting. The turmoil around them can work to strengthen their concentration. In some situations students will practice studying scenes on the streets, trying to spot the threat or potential danger. It might be a suspicious man lurking in an alleyway, a group of restless youths congregating at a street corner, or a figure in a second-story window cradling what might be a high-powered rifle. These are just a few exercises to sharpen your self-defense and observational skills. Military and intelligence agencies are experts in this area of training.

Even though the senses can be sharpened and the powers of observation enhanced, the ability to process information varies with the individual. Two average untrained people who witness the same event are likely to report it differently. This is referred to as "individual perception." In part, previous experiences can determine the manner in which an individual will react to stimuli. People of different ages, cultures, or occupational backgrounds may see the same event very differently. The actual physical processes involved in perception are much the same in every person. But it is the manner in which data is interpreted that determines what a person sees. When it comes to knife fighting, you must attempt to remove preconceived notions, assumptions, and biases that may lead to dangerously incorrect conclusions or oversights. These false reactions form actual blocks to your ability to grasp reality.

Choosing The Right Self-Defense Response

Accurate assessment is critical in knife fighting for two reasons. First, it is imperative that you choose the most appropriate tactical response. There are five possible tactical responses to any particular self-defense situation, listed in order of increasing level of resistance:

- **Comply**
- **Escape**
- **De-escalate**
- **Assert**
- **Fight Back**

Accurate assessment skills will help you choose the appropriate response for the situation.

Comply means to obey the assailant's commands. For example, if you are held at gun point (out of disarming range) for the purpose of robbery, there is nothing to do but comply. Take out your wallet, take off your watch, hand over your car keys, do what you are told. Comply.

Escape or Tactical Retreat means to flee from the threat or danger safely and rapidly. For example, if you are being held hostage and your captor is distracted long enough for you to escape safely, then do it.

De-Escalate means the art and science of diffusing a hostile individual. Not every confrontation warrants fighting back. Often you will be able to use de-escalation skills to talk someone out of a possible violent encounter. An intoxicated loudmouth may be just the type of guy you can settle down and lead away from a problem with effective de-escalation skills.

Assert means standing up for you and your rights. Through effective communication skills you can thwart a person's efforts to intimidate, dominate, and control you. For example, let's say you're working late at the office and your boss makes sexual advances toward you. Now is the time to confront him and be assertive. In a firm and confidant manner, you tell him that you're not interested and that you want him to stop his offensive actions immediately.

Fight Back means using various physical and psychological tactics and techniques to stun, incapacitate, cripple or kill your attacker(s). For example, you're trapped in a dead-end alley by a knife-wielding psychotic who appears determined to butcher you. Your only option is to fight back!

These are just a few of the many possible examples of the five tactical responses. Every self-defense situation is different, and, moreover, most situations can be fluid. A dangerous situation might present an escape option at one moment but quickly turn into a fight-back situation at the next. For example, let's say that you are kidnapped and your captor leaves a door unlocked, and in your effort to escape, you run into him on your way out. Obviously, that is the time to fight for your life.

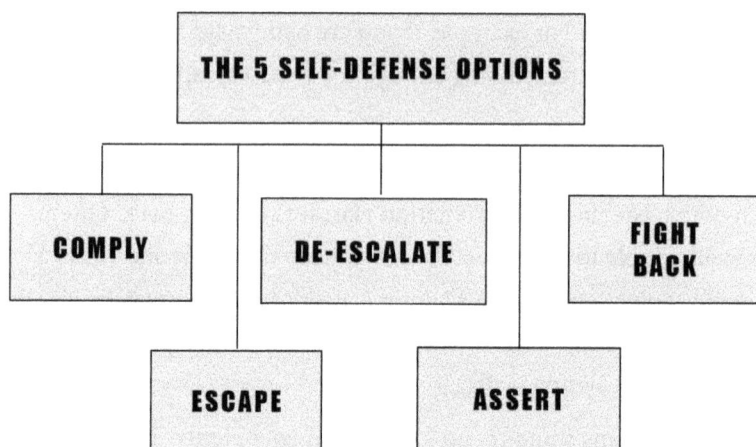

```
                 ┌──────────────────────────────┐
                 │  THE 5 SELF-DEFENSE OPTIONS   │
                 └──────────────────────────────┘
        ┌─────────────────┼─────────────────┐
 ┌────────────┐   ┌────────────────┐   ┌────────────┐
 │   COMPLY   │   │  DE-ESCALATE   │   │   FIGHT    │
 │            │   │                │   │   BACK     │
 └────────────┘   └────────────────┘   └────────────┘
        ┌────────────┐   ┌────────────┐
        │   ESCAPE   │   │   ASSERT   │
        └────────────┘   └────────────┘
```

Avoiding Excessive Force

There is a second important reason why assessment skills are critical in knife fighting: the law. There is an interesting irony facing all law enforcement officers, self-defense, and martial art experts. The more highly trained, knowledgeable, and better you are in knives, combat tactics, martial arts, and other self-defense skills, the higher the standard of care you must observe when protecting yourself or others. If you act too quickly or use what someone might consider "excessive force" in neutralizing an assailant, you may end up being a defendant in a legal process.

America is the most violent society on earth. It is also the most litigious. Most people do not realize that developing a deadly capability to protect yourself carries a tremendous moral and social responsibility. It also involves the risk of civil liability and criminal jeopardy. If you blind or cripple a person, you'd better be prepared to justify this act in the eyes of the law. If you're not careful, you could spend the rest of your life supporting the person who meant to harm you - assuming, of course, that you can get a job once you get out of jail!

The two most popular questions students ask after they have had a little self-defense training are when can you use physical force, and how much physical force is justified? Well, there are no simple answers to these questions. Again, every self-defense situation is different. In one case, a side kick that dislocates an attacker's knee might be judged appropriate force. Change the facts a little and you have a civil battery suit and a criminal charge of aggravated assault. Killing a criminal attacker in one situation may be justified, but a seemingly similar case might result in a civil suit for wrongful death and a criminal charge of manslaughter or murder.

The basic principle is that you must never use force against another person unless it is justified. For civilians, force is broken down into two broad categories: lethal and nonlethal. Any time you use physical force against another person, you run the risk of having a civil suit filed against you. Anyone can hire a lawyer and file a suit for damages. Likewise, anyone can file a criminal complaint against you. Whether criminal charges will be brought against you depends upon the prosecutor or grand jury's views of the facts. No two cases are the same, so there are no easy answers.

I am not qualified to be offering you legal advice. Frankly, I know enough about the law not to make that mistake. However, I can tell you that if you are a highly trained self-defense expert, you will be held to a higher standard of behavior by a jury of your peers. Now there's a good one for you - a jury of your peers. If I ever have to be on trial, I hope that the jury will be comprised of twelve trained self-defense experts. But I won't hold my breath.

A particular troublesome angle to self-defense and legal liability is my first-strike principle (FSP). In many cases, jurors will decide self-defense issues on who struck whom first. That's not good news. My rule is: when faced with a harmful or deadly force situation, and when danger is imminent, then strike first, strike fast, and strike with authority. The problem arises because you may have a hard time justifying your approach in the antiseptic and safe environment of a courtroom many months later. Whenever my life has been in imminent danger, I always acted swiftly. Whether you adopt this approach is entirely up to you.

When to Use Assessment Skills

You should always be alert. Don't become complacent and comfortable. Never assume there is no danger! Learn to assess the situation promptly and accurately, reach a rational conclusion, and choose the appropriate tactical response. The only time you should forget about assessment is when you've been attacked by surprise. For example, a mugger lunges from behind a car, grabs you by the throat, and throws you to the ground. Then it's too late for assessment skills. You must act intuitively and immediately to neutralize him, or you're going to be a statistic. Remember, time is of the essence, and your reaction and reflex must take the place of assessment.

What to Assess

There are two broad factors to assess in a knife fight: the environment and the individual(s). Let's first look at the environment and its related factors.

The Environment

In any knife fighting situation you must strategically evaluate your environment, which is made up of your immediate surroundings. It can be a parking lot, your car, your bedroom, your office, an airport, a park, elevator, nightclub, movie theater, etc. There are four essential factors to consider when assessing your environment. They are escape routes, barriers, makeshift weapons, and terrain. Let's take a look at each one.

Escape routes. These are the various avenues or exits from a threatening situation. Remember, there is nothing cowardly about running away from a knife fight. The ultimate goal of a knife fight is to survive. Some possible escape routes are windows, doors, fire escapes, gates, escalators, fences, walls, bridges, and staircases. But be careful that your version of an escape route doesn't lead you into a worse situation.

Barriers. A barrier is any object that obstructs the attacker's path of attack. At the very least, barriers give you distance and some precious time, and they may give you some safety—at least temporarily. A barrier must have the structural integrity to perform the particular function you have assigned it. Barriers are everywhere and include such things as large desks, doors, automobiles, Dumpsters, large trees, fences, walls, heavy machinery, and large vending machines. The list is endless and depends on the situation, but it is a good idea to assess in advance any possible barriers when entering a potentially hostile or dangerous environment.

Makeshift weapons. These are common, everyday objects that can be converted into offensive and defensive weapons. Like a barrier, a makeshift weapon must be appropriate to the function you have assigned to it. You won't be able to knock someone out with a car antennae, but you could whip it across their eyes and temporarily

Knife Fighting Targets

blind them. Whereas you could knock someone unconscious with a good heavy flashlight but you could not use it to shield yourself from a knife attack.

Makeshift weapons can be broken down into four types: striking, distracting, shielding, and cutting weapons.

Striking makeshift weapons, as the name implies, are objects that can be used to strike an assailant. Examples include heavy flashlights, baseball bats, bottles, beer mugs, text books, binoculars, small lamps, hammers, pool cues, canes, umbrellas, vases, walking sticks, crowbars, light dumbbells, barstools, chairs, etc.

Distracting makeshift weapons are objects that can be thrown at the attacker(s) to temporarily distract him. Depending on the size of the object, a distraction weapon can be thrown into an assailant's face, body, or legs. They include car keys, glass bottles, rolled-up newspaper or magazine, text books, dirt, gravel, sand, hot liquids, spare change, ashtrays, paperweights, wallets, purses, and briefcases. Trash cans, chairs, and bicycles can also be kicked or slammed into an assailant's legs.

Shielding makeshift weapons are objects that temporarily shield you from the assailant's punch, kick, or strike. In some cases, shielding weapons can also be used to protect against knife and bludgeon attacks. Examples of shielding weapons include: trash can lids, briefcases, luggage bags, doors, sofa cushions, thick pillows, ironing boards, hubcaps, food trays, lawn chairs, small tables, backpack, etc.

Cutting makeshift weapons are objects that can be used to cut the assailant by either stabbing or slashing him. Examples include all kitchen cutlery, forks, screwdrivers, broken bottles, broken glass, scissors, car keys, pitch forks, ice scrapers, letter openers, pens, sharp pencils, razor blades, etc. Obviously there is some overlap between the various categories of make-shift weapons. For example, a briefcase can be thrown into an attacker's face for distraction, used to shield against a knife attack, or slammed into an assailant's temple to knock him out.

Terrain. This is a critical environmental factor. What are the strategic implications of the terrain that you are standing on? Will the surface area interfere with your ability to defend against an assailant? Is the terrain wet or dry, mobile or stationary? Obviously, if you are standing on ice, you will be restricted in your efforts to quickly escape or attempt kicking techniques. If the surface is shaky, like a suspension bridge, for example, you may be required to avoid kicking your assailant and instead fight back with hand techniques.

The Individual(s)

Obviously, during a knife fight, you need to assess the source of the threat. Who is posing the possible danger? Is it someone you know or is he a complete stranger? Is it one person or two or more? What are his or her intentions in confronting you with a knife? Pay attention to all available clues, particularly verbal and nonverbal indicators. Let all five of your senses go to work to absorb the necessary information. Also don't forget to listen to what your gut instincts are telling you about the threatening person(s). There are five essential factors to consider when assessing a threatening individual: demeanor, intent, range, positioning, and weapon capability.

Demeanor. In the broadest terms we are talking about the individual's outward behavior. Watch for clues and cues. Is he shaking, or is he calm and calculated? Are his shoulders hunched or relaxed? Are his hands clenched? Is his neck taut? Are his teeth clenched? Is he breathing hard? Does he seem angry or frustrated, or confused and scared? Does he seem high on drugs? Is he mentally ill or simply intoxicated? What is he saying? How is he saying it? Is his speech slurred? What is his tone of voice? Is he talking rapidly or methodically? Is he cursing and angry? All of these verbal and nonverbal cues are essential in assessing the individual's overall demeanor and thus adjusting your tactical response accordingly.

Intent. Once you've got a good read on the assailant's demeanor, you're in a much better position to assess his or her intent. In other words, just what is this person's purpose in confronting you? Does he intend to rob you? Is he seeking retribution for something you have done? Or is he simply looking to frighten you? Determining the individual's intent is perhaps the most important assessment factor, but it can also be the most difficult. Moreover, when it comes to criminal intent, things can change pretty quickly. For example, an intent to rob can quickly turn into an intent to rape. In any event, the appropriate tactical response is highly dependent upon a correct assessment of intent.

Range. Range is the spatial relationship between you and the assailant(s) in terms of distance. In knife fighting, there are three general distances from which fight: long, intermediate, and close-quarter. I'll talk more about knife fighting ranges in Chapter 3.

When assessing a threatening individual, you'll need to recognize the strategic implications of his range. For example, how close is he from delivering a cut? Is he at a distance from which he could stab you? Is he in a range that allows him to grab hold of your knife, or take you to the ground? Is he moving through the ranges of knife combat? If so, how fast? Does he continue to move forward when you step back?

Positioning. This is the spatial relationship of the assailant(s) to you in terms of threat, escape, and target selection. Are you surrounded by multiple assailants or only one? Is he standing squarely or sideways, above or below you? What anatomical targets does the assailant present you with? Is he blocking the door or any other avenue of escape? Is his back to the light source? Is he close to your only makeshift weapon? You must answer these questions before choosing a tactical strategy appropriate to the situation.

Weapon capability. Is your assailant armed or unarmed? If he is carrying a weapon, what type is it? Does he have a delivery method for the particular weapon? Is he armed with more than one weapon? Sometimes it is easy to determine if someone is armed. For example, you see a knife sheath on his belt. At other times your assessment skills need to be more advanced. For example, is the person wearing a jacket when it is too hot for a jacket? Could it be to conceal a knife at the waist? Is the person patting his chest? When scanning the person, can you see his hands and all his fingertips? Is one hand behind him or in his pockets? Could he be palming a knife or some other edged weapon? Are his arms crossed? Does he seem to be reaching for something? Does he seem suspiciously rooted to a particular spot? Is his body language incongruous with his verbal cues you are reading? The CFA rule: When you're not certain, always assume your assailant is armed with a weapon.

Controlling Fear

To the untrained person, any kind of violent encounter (especially a knife fight) will result in some level of fear. Fear is a strong and unpleasant emotional reaction to a real or perceived threat. If uncontrolled, fear leads to panic. Then it's too late to adequately protect yourself.

The Three Levels of Fear

To prevent the negative effects of fear during a knife fight, you need to understand its levels and dynamics. For analysis, I have categorized fear into three different levels, listed in order of intensity:

Knife Fighting Targets

- Fright (quick or sudden fear)
- Panic (overpowering fear)
- Terror (crippling or immobilizing fear)

While these three levels of fear vary in degrees of stress, they all have one common root response: the fight-or-flight response.

What is The Fight-or-Flight Response?

Whenever a person, or any animal for that matter, feels threatened or frightened, certain physiological changes occur. They start in the brain when the hypothalamus sends strong impulses to the pituitary gland, causing it to release a hormone (ACTH) that stimulates the adrenal glands to release other hormones into the bloodstream.

Ultimately every nerve and muscle is involved. This adrenaline will cause an increased heart rate with a corresponding increase in respiration and blood pressure. Your muscles will tense up, you will start to sweat, and your mouth will go dry. In addition, your digestive system will shut down to allow a better supply of blood to the muscles. Your hair will stand on end (piloerection). Your pupils will enlarge so that your vision can improve. Your hand and limbs will also begin to tremble. Once these biochemical mechanisms and processes are fully engaged - and it takes only nanoseconds - your body will be in the fight-or-flight mode.

For most people, the fight-or-flight response has a debilitating effect. They panic or freeze up, and fear then becomes a powerful weapon of the attacker. By paralyzing you with fear, his job is easier. Therefore, it is critically important that you learn to control the fight-or-flight response to make it work for you and not against you during a knife fight.

First, accept the fact that the fight-or-flight response is a natural human response. In fact, it's one of Mother Nature's best ways of helping you survive a dangerous situation. You've got to take advantage of this assistance by using the energy of the adrenaline surge to augment your counterattack and awaken your killer instinct. The killer instinct burns on the fuel of adrenaline and can be a vicious and lethal source of energy. Properly channeled, this destructiveness will exceed that of your assailant, and you will overwhelm him.

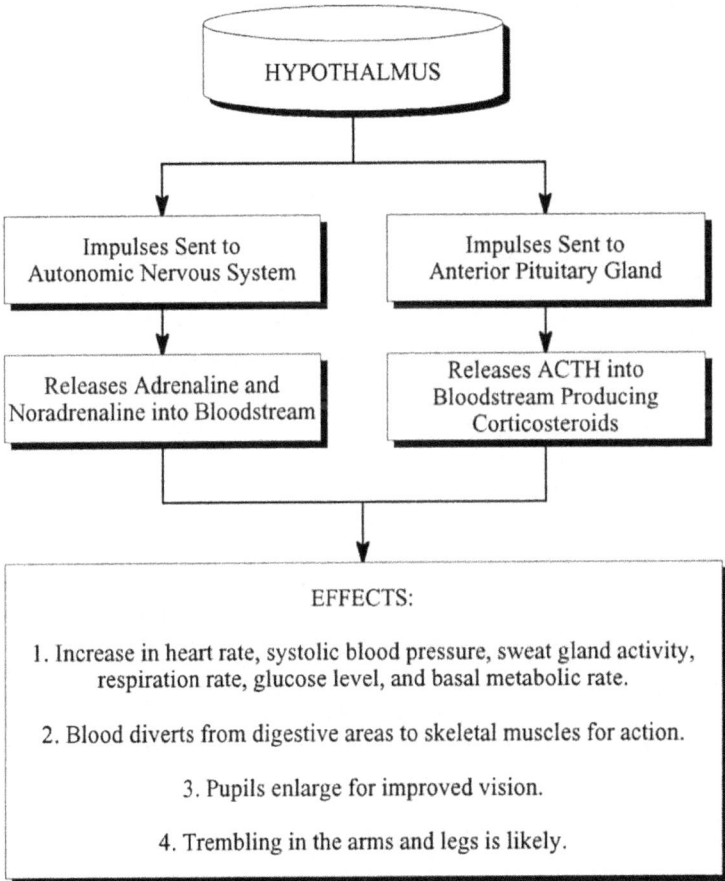

HYPOTHALMUS

Impulses Sent to Autonomic Nervous System	Impulses Sent to Anterior Pituitary Gland
Releases Adrenaline and Noradrenaline into Bloodstream	Releases ACTH into Bloodstream Producing Corticosteroids

EFFECTS:

1. Increase in heart rate, systolic blood pressure, sweat gland activity, respiration rate, glucose level, and basal metabolic rate.

2. Blood diverts from digestive areas to skeletal muscles for action.

3. Pupils enlarge for improved vision.

4. Trembling in the arms and legs is likely.

Pictured here, a diagram of the fight-or-flight response.

Knife Fighting Targets

Second, harness the fight-or-flight response by preparing yourself thoroughly for the danger that may one day confront you. Developing the psychological and physical skills of knife fighting will lead to a personal self-confidence. In turn, this confidence leads to an inner calm. Inner calm is the environment necessary to the killer instinct, and the killer instinct will drink adrenaline like a race horse drinks water.

Your preparation involves learning the physical skills, techniques, and tactics required to use your knife effectively. The only way to achieve these skills and techniques is with lots of study and practice.

This type of physical training leads to psychological preparedness. Once you begin to understand what a knife fight consists of, you can expand your training to visualize such confrontations and the necessary control over the fight-or-flight syndrome.

You must continue to develop this keen sense of self-awareness to be psychologically prepared for a violent confrontation. Never stop assessing your state of mind and reactions to different stressful situations. For example, the next time you are startled by something, pay close attention. What was it that startled you and why? Did you freeze up? What did you see? What did you hear? Were you trembling and breathing heavily? Was your mind clear or distracted? Exactly what were you thinking about? How much detail can you remember? Did you make any tactical errors in your responses? These are only a few of the questions you should answer over and over again as you go through the process of preparing yourself psychologically.

Another method of psychological preparation is written analysis. For example, write down five different hypothetical scenarios (i.e., carjacking, robbery, rape attempt, etc.) that truly frighten you. These scenarios could take place anywhere (home, workplace, street, hiking trail, parking lot). Be specific with your details. Make certain to include the following relevant factors:

- Time of day
- Environment
- Attacker's description
- Number of attackers
- Type of crime
- Assailant's intent
- Type of physical attack/assault
- Type of weapon
- Your immediate physical condition at time of attack
- Any other relevant factors to your scenario

Once you've completed these scenarios, identify the specific factors that elicit reasonable fear and then adjust your knife fighting training to meet your concerns.

In the interim, if you find yourself in a knife fight and cannot control your fight-or-flight response and you become overwhelmed with panic, quickly convert your fear into raw, vicious anger. That's right: get mad! Some low-life thug is about to injure or kill you or some loved one. Tear him apart. Relying purely on anger is not the best way of defending yourself, but your raw anger can still be a powerful emotion that can be used in your favor.

Possible Physiological Responses To Fear

- Enlarged pupils
- Dry mouth
- Trembling hands
- Cold, clammy hands
- Increased heart rate
- Shutdown of digestive system

Knife Fighting Targets

- Tense muscles
- Sudden adrenaline surge
- Hair stands on end
- Enhanced alertness

How To Control Your Fear During a Knife Fight

Here are a few suggestions that will help you control the deleterious effects of fear:

- Learn the necessary skills and tactics of knife fighting.

- Be confident and competent with your weapon skills.

- Regularly practice knife fighting rehearsal (visualization) scenarios.

- Understand and accept the physiological responses to the fight-or-flight response.

- Learn how to tap and control your killer instinct.

- Evaluate your past responses to dangerous or threatening situations.

- Learn the differences between "perceptual danger" and "reasonable danger."

- Always believe in your knife fighting skills and abilities.

- Always trust your instincts and judgments.

- Develop accurate threat assessment skills.

- Adopt the will to survive.

- Always strive to be physically fit.

- Maintain a high degree of situational awareness.

- Always keep a positive mental attitude.

Chapter 2
Knife Fighting Checklist

Knife Fighting Targets

What You Must Know

In order to benefit from the knife targeting techniques featured in the next chapter, you must first have a solid understanding of the basic knife fighting fundamentals. They include:

- **Knife Selection**
- **Knife Grips and Ranges**
- **Stances and Footwork**
- **Cuts and Angles of Attack**
- **Angles of Attack**
- **Knife Fighting Strategies**
- **Knife Fighting Training**

This book already assumes you have a decent foundation in basic knife fighting skills. Regardless of your skill level, I will briefly cover two critical two concepts that are germane to knife targeting. They are **knife grips** and **knife fighting ranges**.

The knife fighting grips

One of the foundational elements of knife fighting is the grip. When I say, "grip," I am referring to how the knife is held and manipulated in your hand during a knife fight. When it comes to tactical knife combat, the grip should accomplish the following three objectives.

1. **Provides positive weapon retention** – The ability to hold on to your knife in the heat of battle is vital. This is especially important when your hands are sweaty or covered with blood. Remember, never pick up a knife unless you are confident that you can maintain complete control of it at all times. In Contemporary Fighting Arts, I have a saying, "Lose your weapon and you lose your life."

2. **Permits effective use and manipulation** – The ability to maneuver and manipulate your blade goes without saying. Remember, a knife is a multi-directional weapon designed to change angles of attack in a split second.

3. **Helps manages shock impact** – If your blade hits bone you better have a grip that will manage the impact shock. Remember, cutting the air with your knife is nothing like making hard contact with flesh and bone.

When gripping your knife, always make certain that the cutting edge faces your assailant. I know this may seem obvious to some of you, but you would be amazed how many people make the mistake of facing the blade edge the wrong way. Also, be very careful not to wrap your fingers too tightly around the handle. This can be dangerous for the following reasons:

1. It restricts wrist mobility.

2. It reduces your slashing and stabbing speed.

3. It weakens your forearm muscles.

4. It creates greater target exposure by forcing your veins to protrude from your hands and forearms.

As you can imagine, there are a variety of different gripping techniques you can use during a knife fight. Depending on the circumstance, each grip will have advantages and disadvantages. Just remember that *you must always choose the appropriate grip for the particular knife range.* For example, if you were knife fighting at long range, you wouldn't use an ice pick grip. Instead, you would opt for the hammer or saber grip.

A skilled technician should be well versed in the different knife grips and, if necessary, capable of switching hand grips safely and efficiently.

The four primary knife fighting grips include the following:

*   Hammer grip
*   Saber grip
*   Ice pick
*   Modified ice pick

Let's take a closer look at each one.

Hammer Grip

The hammer grip is the same type of grip you would use if you were holding an actual hammer. Hence, the name - hammer grip.

Generally, when performing the hammer grip, the exposed area of the blade will be seen above your thumb line. The hammer grip can be used for both quick slashing and powerful stabbing techniques and it can be used in long, intermediate, and close quarter knife fighting ranges.

Pictured here, the hammer grip which can be used for both slashing and stabbing techniques.

Saber Grip

With the saber grip, you would hold the knife in the same way that you would hold a saber sword, with the thumb extended forward on the top of the handle.

Since the thumb positioning of the saber grip alleviates pressure on your wrist, it's a very comfortable grip for delivering linear thrusts to selected targets.

Like the hammer grip, the saber grip can also be used for both quick slashing and powerful stabbing techniques and it can be used in long, intermediate, and close quarter knife fighting ranges.

Pictured here, the saber grip.

Knife Fighting Targets

Ice-Pick Grip

Next, is the ice pick grip. As you can imagine, this grip is similar to holding an ice pick in your hand. Generally, the exposed area of the blade will be seen below your pinky finger.

This grip should be used when knife fighting at close-quarters or on the ground. Because of the limited reach of the blade, do not use this grip at long knife fighting range.

Like the hammer grip, the ice pick grip can also be used for both slashing and stabbing movements. However, sufficient wrist flexibility is required to perform many ice pick slashing movements. So, if you do have *tight* wrists, you might want to practice slashing movements with the ice pick grip until your wrists loosen up and your technique becomes fast and fluid.

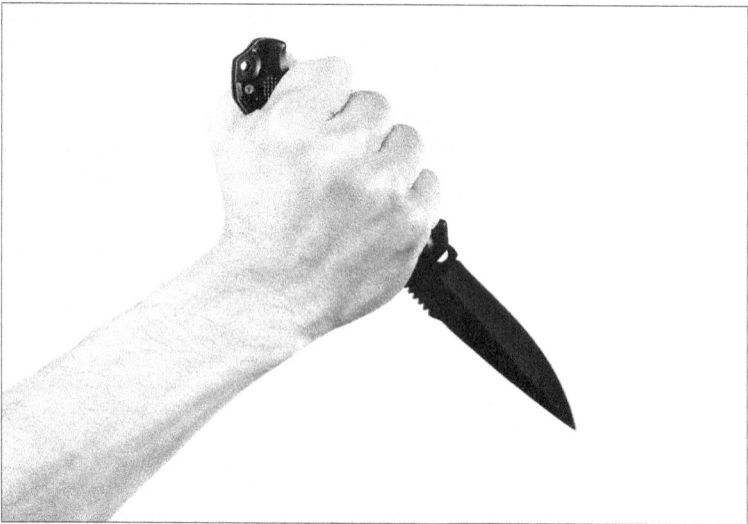

Pictured here, the ice pick grip which can be used for both slashing and stabbing techniques.

Knife Palming with the Ice Pick grip

The ice pick grip also permits you to palm your knife in your hand. *Knife palming* is a strategic method of concealing your knife behind your forearm during the precontact stage of knife fighting.

Knife palming is probably one of the most deceptive forms of knife concealment and can surprise even the most seasoned knife fighter. Therefore, when confronted by a potential adversary, always be aware of his hands. Remember, if you can't see the opponent's fingertips, beware - he could also be palming a knife.

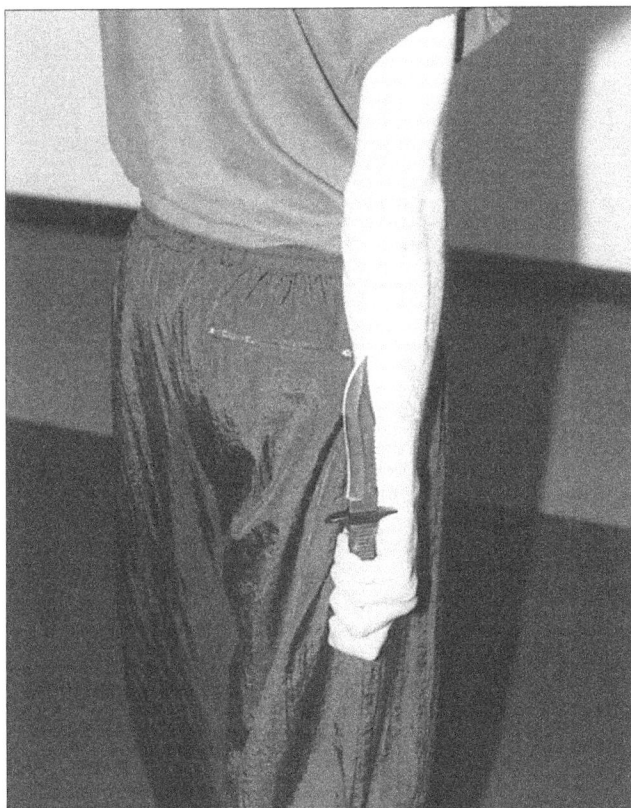

Pictured here, the deceptive knife palming technique.

Knife Fighting Targets

The knife fighting grips are not just limited to knife fighting. They have numerous weapon applications, including the ubiquitous tactical pen.

When using the ice pick grip, don't make the novice mistake of holding the knife with the cutting edge facing away from the adversary.

Modified Ice Pick Grip

To apply this grip, hold your knife in the ice pick grip with your thumb placed firmly on the butt of the weapon. Once again, the exposed area of the blade will be seen below your pinky.

Capping the butt of the knife is especially important because it helps reinforce your grip on the knife. This allows you to deliver full-force stabbing movements without dislodging the weapon from your hand and possibly slicing your fingers.

Because of the limited reach of the blade, do not use this grip at long knife fighting range.

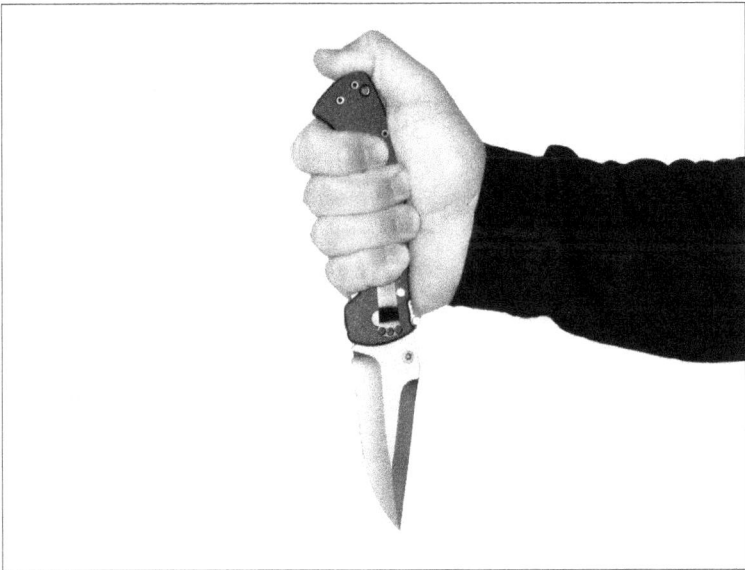

Pictured here, the modified ice pick grip.

Other knife grips

As you might imagine, there are many other grips available to a knife fighter. For example, the Filipino grip where your thumb rides on the spine of the blade. Or the scalpel grip, where your index finger extends along the spine of the blade, much the same way a surgeon holds a scalpel during surgery. And there are others like the foil and two finger grips.

While these exotic knife grips are unique and might serve some utility, they compromised the structural integrity of your grip making them inherently risky for real-world knife fighting applications. So, if you are serious about surviving a knife fight, stick to the four tried-and-true grips that will save your life when the chips are down: hammer, saber, ice pick and modified ice pick.

Pictured here, the scalpel grip. Do you see any flaws with this type of grip?

Switching knife grips

As I said earlier, a skilled knife fighter should be proficient with the various types of knife grips and capable of switching these grips as his or her situation demands.

Grip switching is an invaluable knife fighting skill that will can be developed with regular practice. If you are new to grip switching, I strongly encourage you to practice this skill with a safety training knife first. Only after you have mastered the technique should you practice with a real knife.

Keep in mind that grip switching will be problematic if you are using the following types knives:

- Knuckle knives

- Trench knives

- Deep finger grooved knives

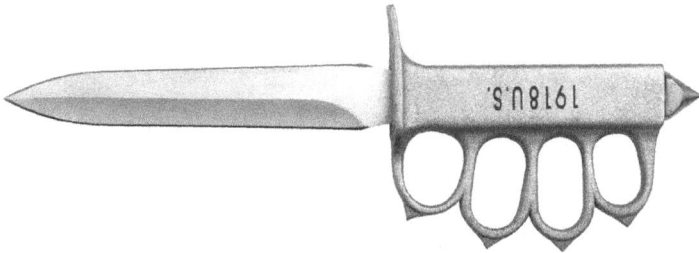

Grip switching is invaluable during a knife fight, so you will want to avoid using knuckle, trench, and finger grooves knives.

Switching from hammer to ice pick grips

By far, the most important grip switching sequence is changing the knife from a hammer or saber grip to an ice pick grip. What follows is the counter-clockwise switching technique.

Step 1: Begin by holding the knife in either a hammer or saber grip.

Step 2: With the knife pointing forward, turn the knife counter-clockwise in the palm of your hand.

Step 3: Next, pivot the rear portion of the handle in the palm of your hand so the spine of the blade swings back.

Step 4: The knife should be secure in your hand with an ice pick grip.

Clockwise Method

If you prefer, you can also switch knife grips by using the clockwise method.

Step 1: Begin by holding the knife in either a hammer or saber grip.

Step 2: With the knife pointing forward, turn the knife clockwise in the palm of your hand.

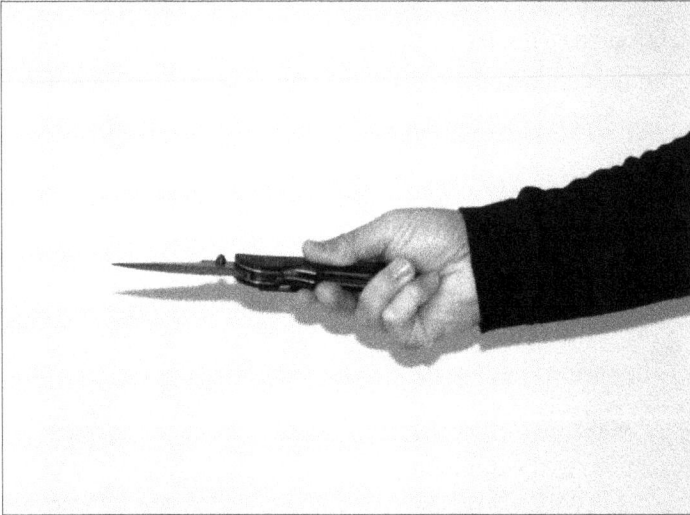

Step 3: Next, pivot the rear portion of the handle in the palm of your hand so the front of the blade swings back.

Step 4: The knife should be secure in your hand with an ice pick grip.

Grip Orientation Drill

It's important that your knife grips are second nature and can be readily applied under the duress of a knife fight. Here's a grip orientation drill that will make the knife grips instinctual.

1. Begin from a knife fighting stance.

2. Place your knife in your lead dominant hand.

3. Next, have your training partner randomly call out the various knife grips.

4. Quickly and smoothly configure the different grips at the pace of the commands.

5. Perform this exercise for five minutes.

6. Switch hands and start again for another five minutes.

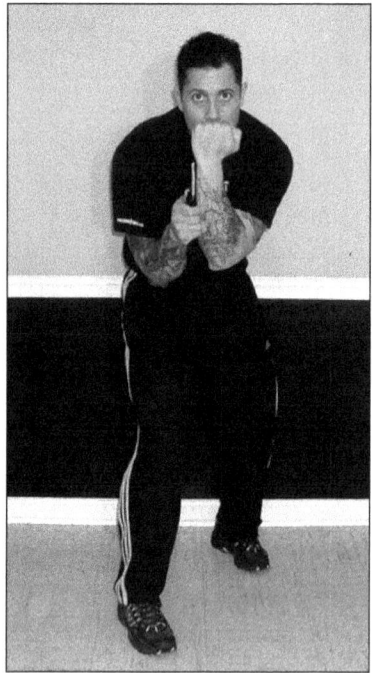

Once you have this drill down, have your partner increase the cadence of the verbal commands while you perform the exercise with your eyes closed. This is extremely beneficial because it will help you develop a kinesthetic feel for the different knife grips.

Grip Switching Drill

The grip switching drill is ideal for making your switching technique quick and fluid. Again, I strongly encourage you to start off with a safety training knife, and then progress to using a real blade.

1. Begin from a knife fighting stance.

2. Place your knife in your lead dominant hand.

3. Assume the hammer or saber grip.

4. Next, have you training partner call out "switch."

5. Using either the clockwise of counter-clockwise method, quickly and smoothly switch to the ice pick grip

6. Again, have your partner call out "switch."

7. Reverse the switching sequence so you knife is back to the hammer or saber grip.

8. Be certain to maintain a solid knife fighting stance throughout the duration of the exercise.

9. Continue this drill for a period of five to ten minutes.

10. Switch your stance and hands and start again for another five to ten minutes.

Hand Switching during a knife fight

As I will be discussing in the next chapter, you always want to hold your knife in your front dominant hand during a knife fighting.

However, some knife fighting instructors advocate hand switching with your knife for a variety of different reasons. Some include countering an opponent's disarm, evading a trap, or possibly exploiting a vulnerable target from the other side.

I categorically disagree! *Hand switching during a knife fight is extremely risky and should be avoided as much as possible.* The only time you should switch hands is when you knife wielding hand is injured to the point where you can no longer use the weapon effectively.

Knife fighting ranges

Knife fighting is fluid and dynamic and will often force you and your adversary to move in and out of ranges of engagement. In order to survive the knife fight, you must be proficient in all three ranges of knife combat. Remember, just like unarmed combat, you never know which range you will be forced to engage with the adversary. So you must be prepared for all of them.

As I stated earlier, knife fighting ranges are directly linked to knife grips and *you must always choose the appropriate grip for the knife fighting range.*

You must choose the appropriate grip for the knife fighting range. Pictured here, the fighter on the left has a clear reach advantage over his adversary.

The three knife fighting range include long, intermediate, and close-quarter distances. Let's start by taking a look at the long range of knife fighting.

Long range

This is the farthest distance of knife fighting where you can only reach and cut your opponent's hand or wrist flexor. The hammer grip or saber grip are ideal for this range of combat.

The long range of knife fighting.

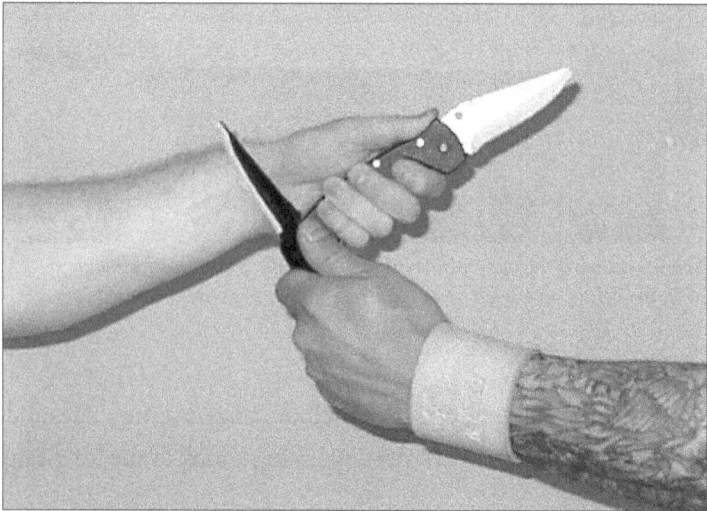

The opponent's wrist flexor is your primary target at this range.

Intermediate range

Next, we have the intermediate range of knife fighting. At this distance you are close enough to cut the mid to upper portion of the opponent's arm (from his wrist flexor to the upper biceps) as well as torso and head targets. For the advantages of maximum reach, the hammer and saber grips are preferred for this distance.

Pictured here, the intermediate knife fighting range.

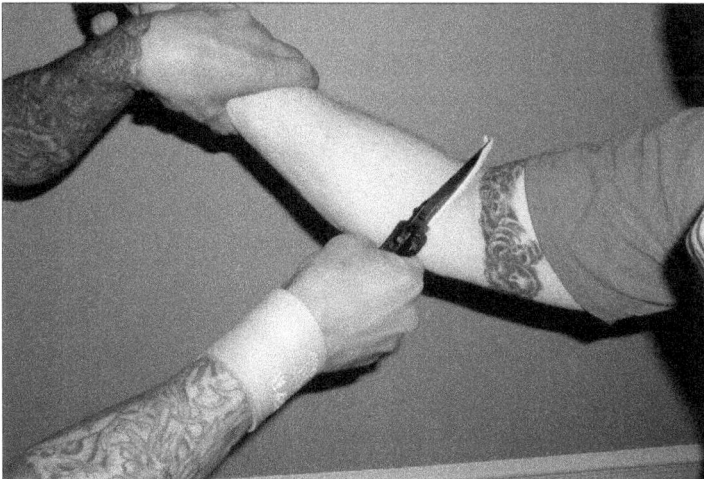

The biceps is an ideal target at the intermediate range.

69

Close Quarter range

At this distance, you are close enough to stab the opponent's body with either the ice pick or modified ice pick grips. Other secondary close-quarter knife combat techniques can also be applied (i.e., head butt, biting tactics, elbow strikes, etc).

Close-quarter knife fighting can also take place on the ground. Keep in mind that ground fighting with edged weapons is a treacherous task reserved for only the most skilled knife fighter.

The close-quarter range of knife combat.

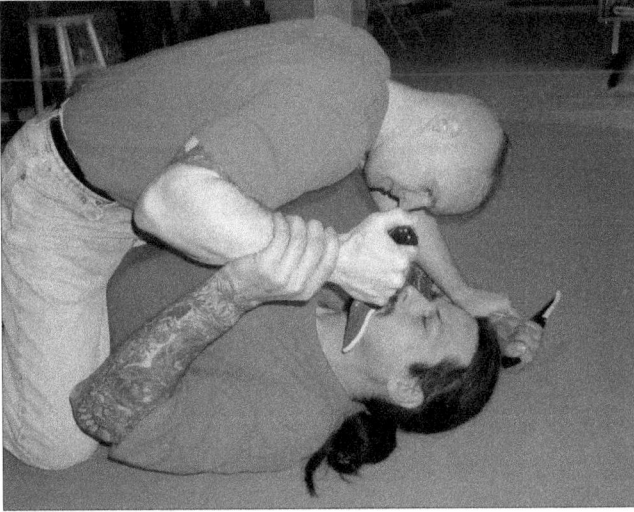

Pictured here, close-quarter knife fighting on the ground.

Knife Fighting Targets

Chapter 3
Knife Fighting Targets

Knife Fighting Targets

Knife Target Classifications

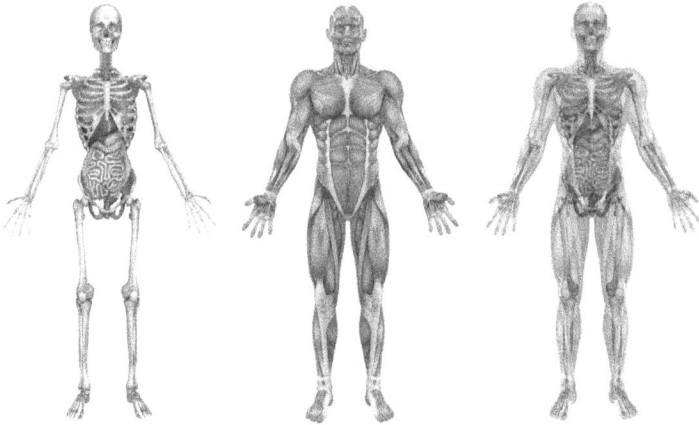

The reality of knife fighting is that it's fast, furious and often fatal, so you must do as much damage as quickly as possible. Therefore, a skilled knife fighter should only seek out anatomical targets that produce the greatest amount of damage and shock.

Moreover, anyone who chooses to use a knife for self-defense has both a legal and moral responsibility to know the medical implications of every target. A competent blade fighter must know exactly which anatomical targets will shock, maim, immobilize, and kill the adversary.

To help you better understand the concept of knife targeting, I've classified all of the essential anatomical targets into one of three distinct categories. They are:

- Immobilizers
- Bleeders
- Quick Kills

Knife Fighting Targets

However, target classifications are not mutually exclusive. For example, a bleeder target, like the brachial artery, is also considered an immobilizer target when the limb becomes inoperable from a knife cut.

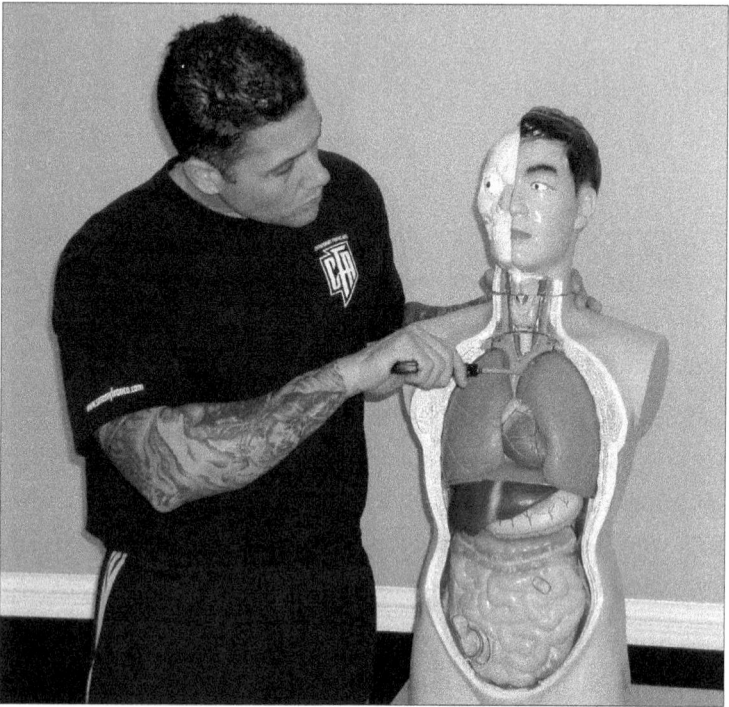

Knife fighting is a deadly business. Here, Sammy Franco discusses knife targets with some of his students.

Immobilizer targets

Immobilizers are anatomical targets that hinder or immobilize the assailant's limbs. It can be muscle and nerve tissue, tendons, ligaments, and certain connective tissue.

For example, if you slash the back of the opponent's knee, you would be attacking an immobilization target the will prevent the adversary from using his afflicted leg. Generally, attacking an immobilizer targets will often leave the adversary crippled for life.

The primary immobilizer target in both long and intermediate knife range is the assailant's wrist flexor (the one that is holding the knife). If you slash this target with sufficient force, the opponent will most likely drop his weapon and lose complete use of his knife wielding hand. This knife fighting strategy will be discussed in greater depth in Chapter 7.

This critical knife fighting strategy is most commonly called "defanging the snake." Meaning, if you cut your opponent's knife hand where he can no longer hold his weapon, then you've essentially removed the fangs from a deadly snake. Other Immobilizer targets will include:

- Hand tendons
- Wrists
- Forearm flexors
- Biceps
- Triceps
- Back of knee
- Achilles tendon
- Any joint region

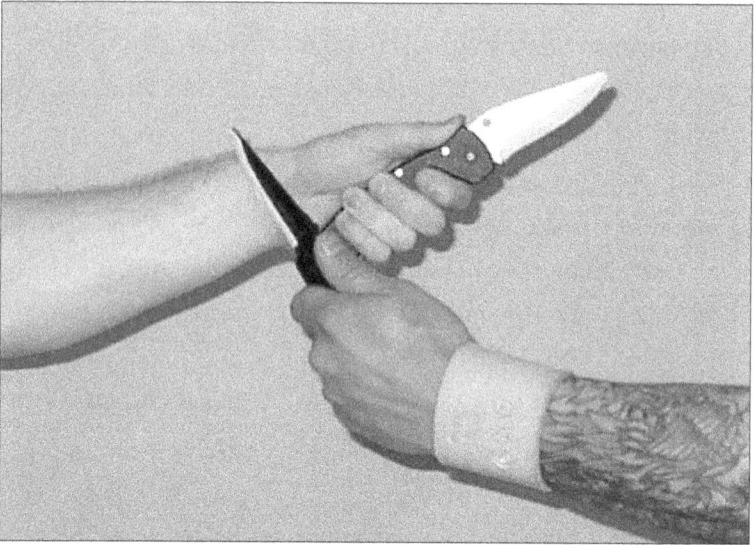

The number one immobilizer target during a knife fight is the opponent's wrist.

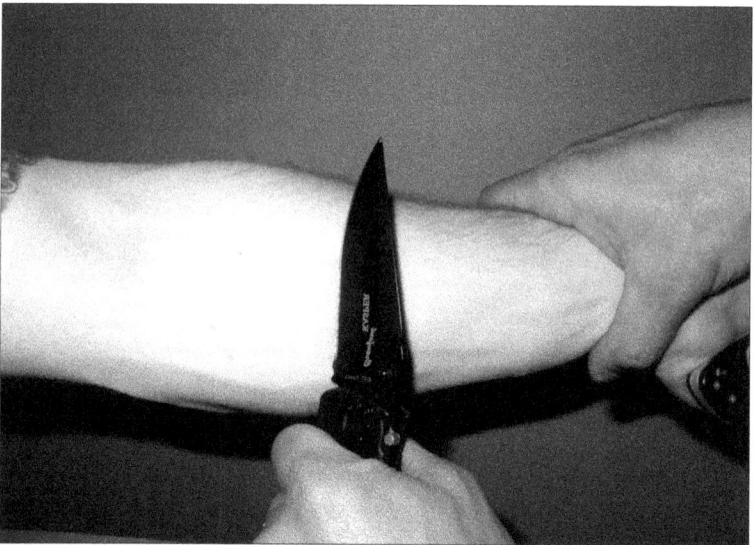

Provided your cut is deep enough, the forearm is another vulnerable immobilizer target.

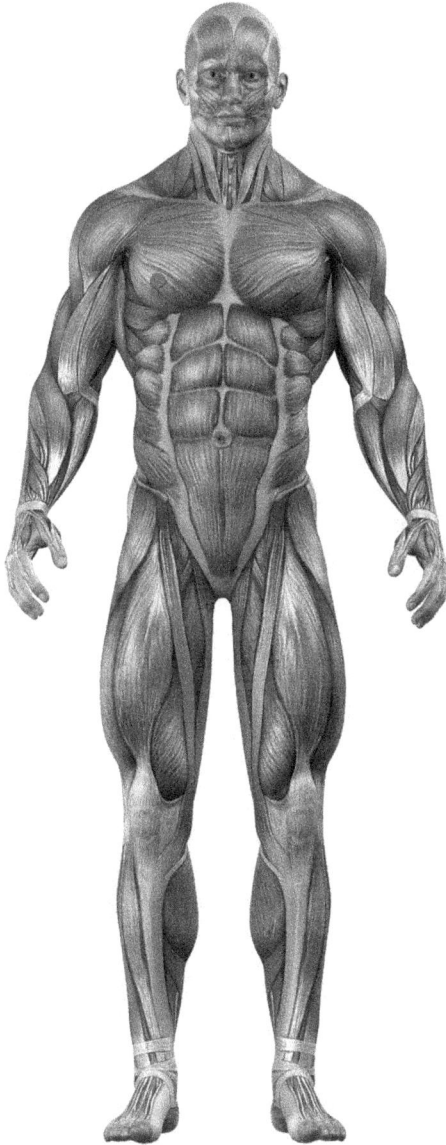

Immobilizers are anatomical targets that hinder or immobilize the assailant's limbs. It can be muscle and nerve tissue, tendons, ligaments and certain connective tissue.

Knife Fighting Targets

If you are solo training, you can use the Bob Jacket to work on immobilizer knife targets.

Bleeder targets (attacking the arterial system)

Bleeders are anatomical targets that directly impact the enemy's cardiovascular system. Since arteries lead oxygenated blood away from your heart, they are under tremendous pressure. If you slash or stab one of these arteries, you will cause rapid blood loss that will put an end to the confrontation.

Cutting the assailant's arteries is not as easy as you think. The walls of the human artery are thick, resilient and usually protected by tendons and muscle tissue. It will take substantial cutting force to get at them!

Loss of consciousness or death from an arterial bleeder will depend on many factors, such as the enemy's pulse rate, level of conditioning, location of cut, depth of cut, and the type of cut.

In most cases, arterial bleeders will cause loss of consciousness (due to rapid blood pressure loss) before death. Bleeder targets include the following:

- Carotid artery
- Brachial artery
- Radial artery
- Ulnar artery
- Axillary artery
- Femoral artery

Knife Fighting Targets

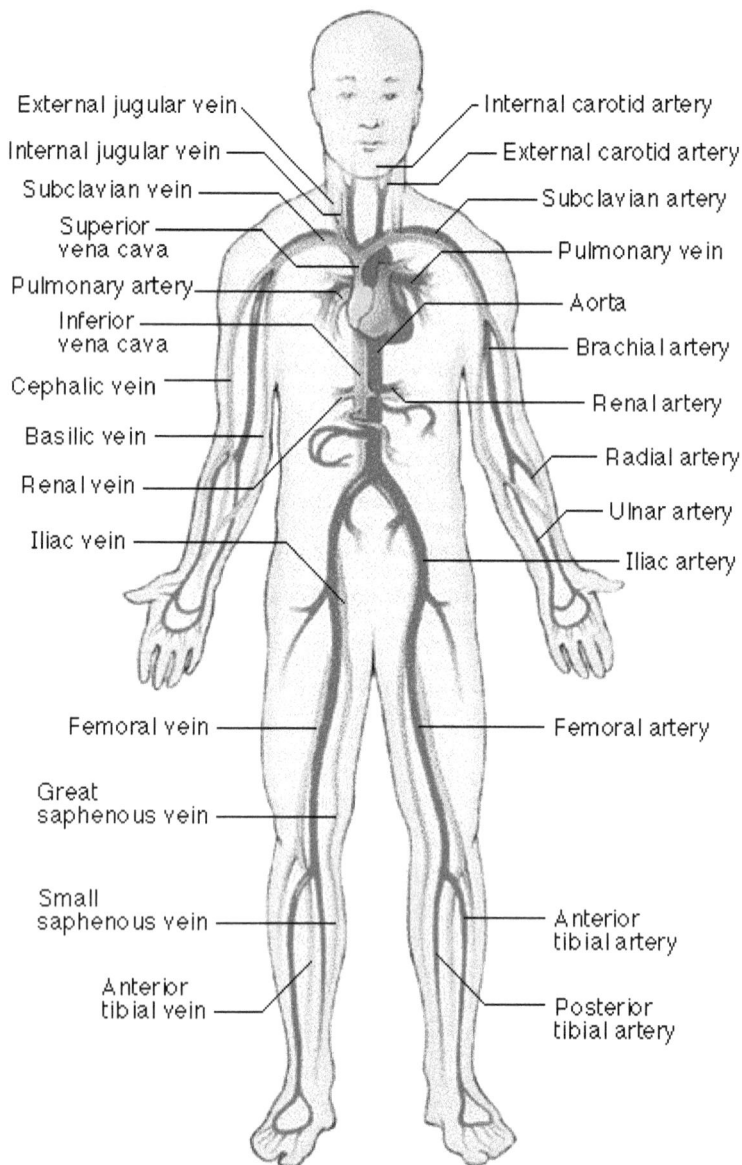

External jugular vein

Internal jugular vein

Subclavian vein

Superior vena cava

Pulmonary artery

Inferior vena cava

Cephalic vein

Basilic vein

Renal vein

Iliac vein

Femoral vein

Great saphenous vein

Small saphenous vein

Anterior tibial vein

Internal carotid artery

External carotid artery

Subclavian artery

Pulmonary vein

Aorta

Brachial artery

Renal artery

Radial artery

Ulnar artery

Iliac artery

Femoral artery

Anterior tibial artery

Posterior tibial artery

The human circulatory system.

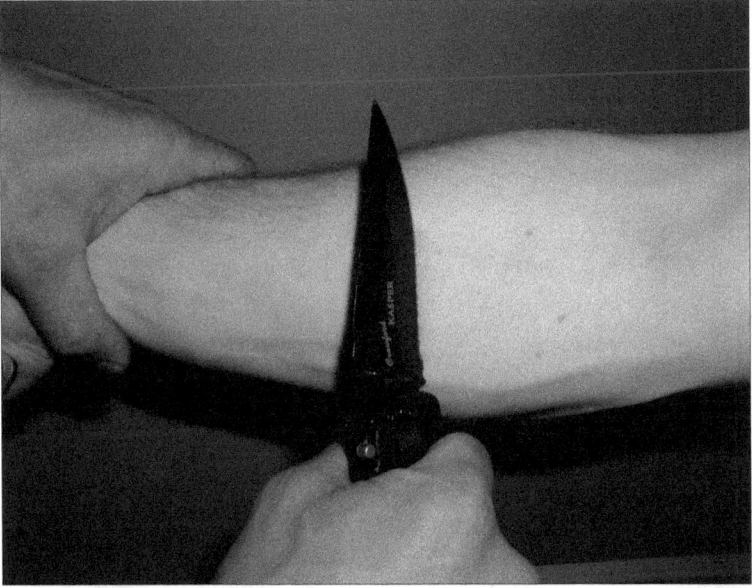

Bleeder target: Ulnar and Radial arteries.

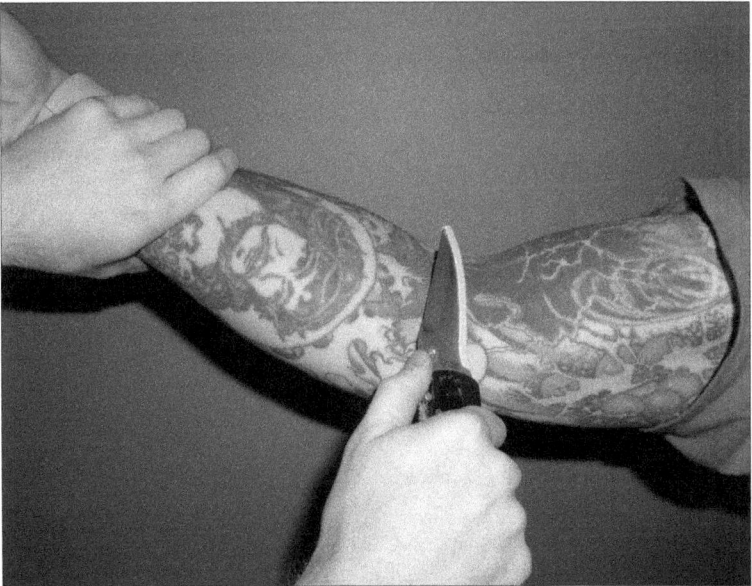

Bleeder target: Brachial artery.

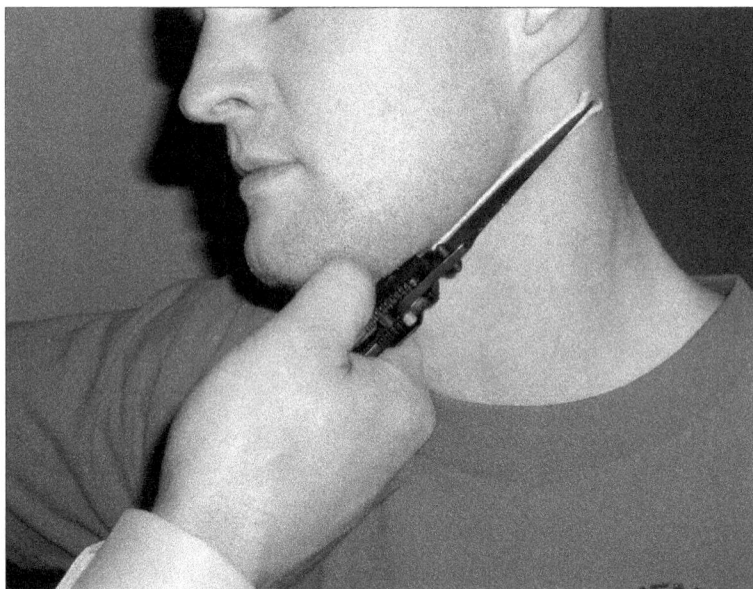

Bleeder target: Carotid artery.

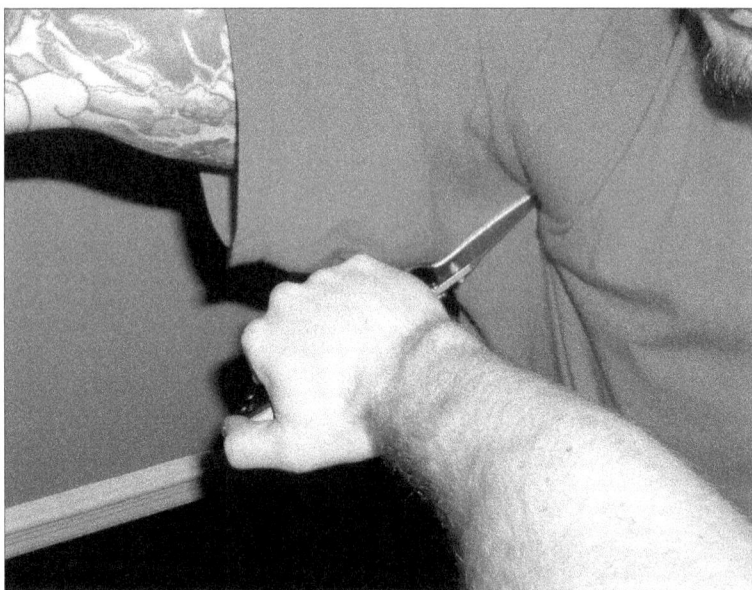

Bleeder target: Axillary artery.

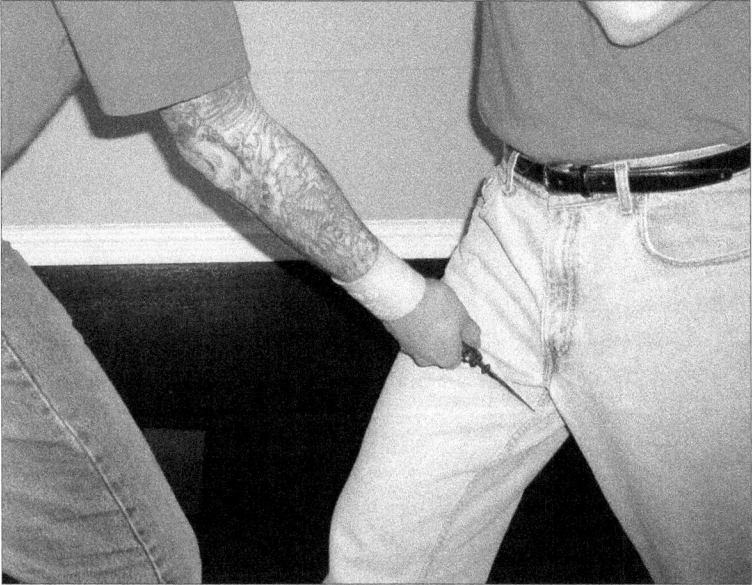

Bleeder target: Femoral artery.

Quick Kill targets

Quick kills are the most lethal knife fighting targets. In most cases, one deliberate cut to a quick kill target will immediately end the knife fight. Generally, a quick kill attack is usually delivered in a stabbing motion, yet there are always exceptions.

Just as there are quick kill targets on the adversary, they are also present on you. You must be very careful not to expose a quick kill target to your enemy. This is why I place so much emphasis on mastering a solid knife fighting stance.

Quick kill targets include the following:

- Eye socket
- Heart
- Lateral side of the head
- Subclavian arteries
- Back of neck
- Groin
- Ear canal
- Throat

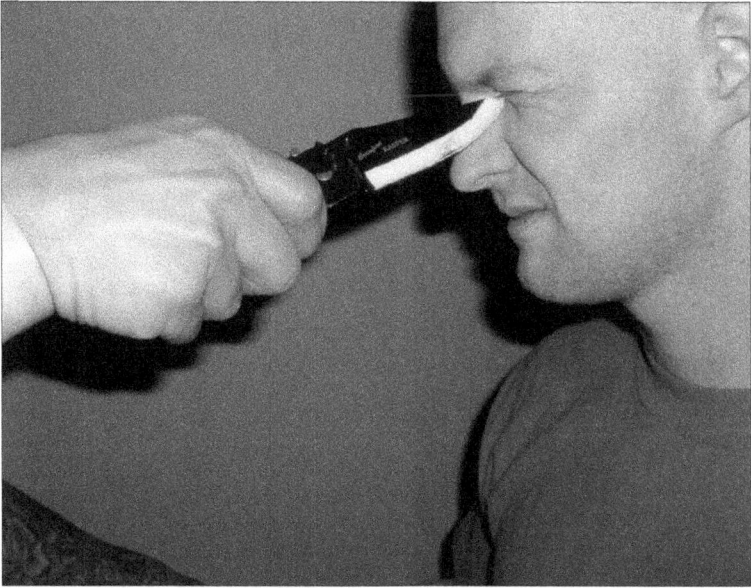

Quick kill target: the eye socket.

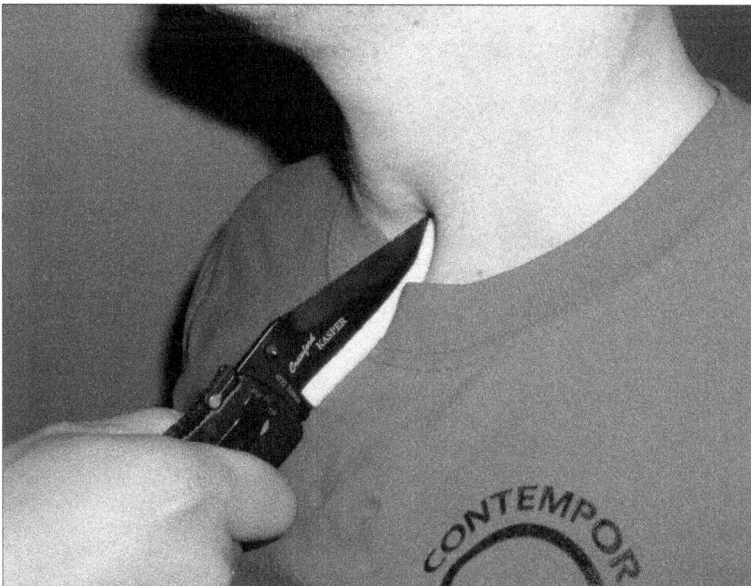

Quick kill target: the throat.

Knife Fighting Targets

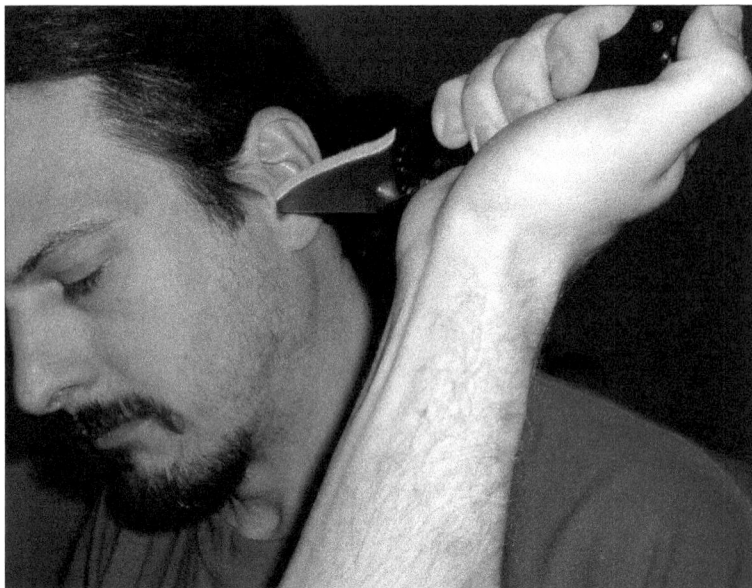

Quick kill target: the ear canal.

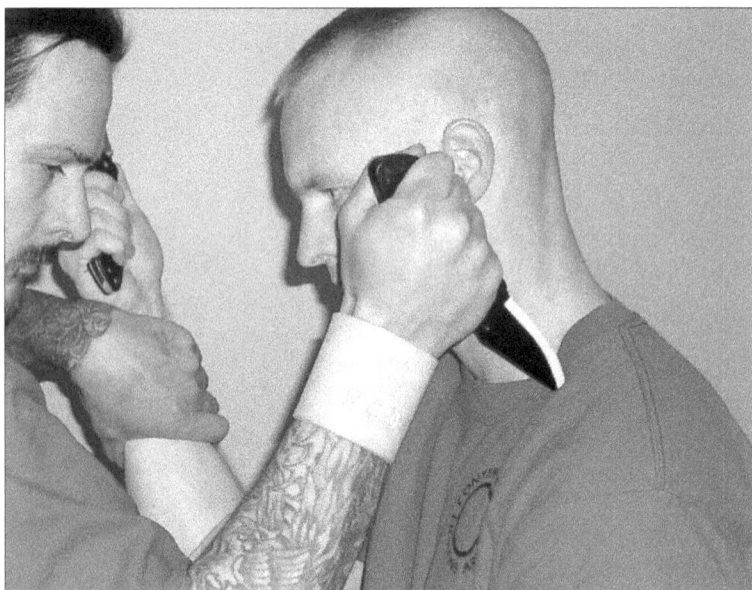

Quick kill target: Subclavian artery.

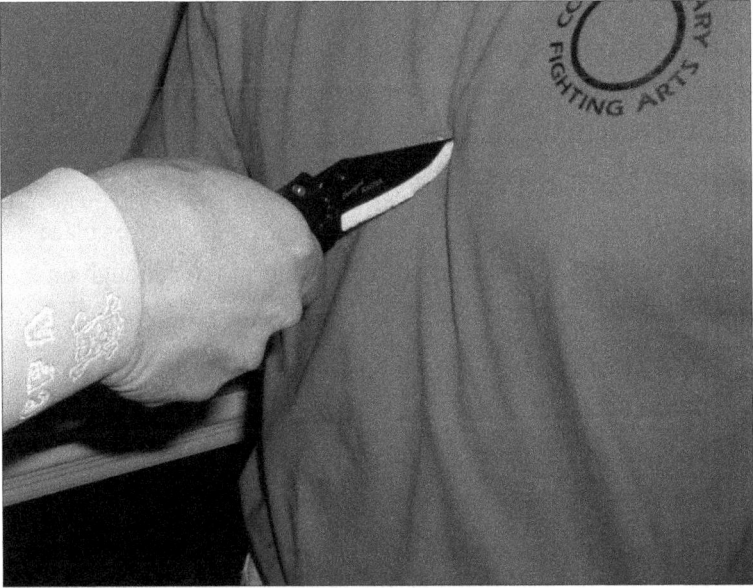

Quick kill target: Heart.

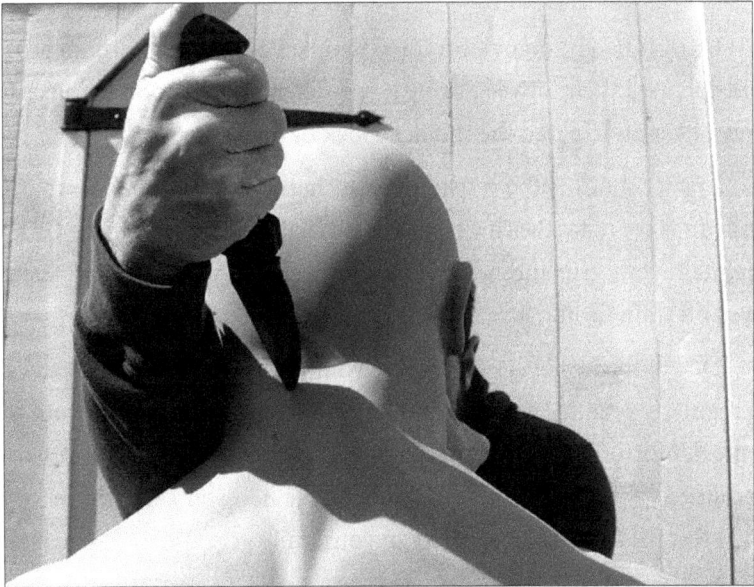

Quick kill target: Back of Neck

Impact Shock when Cutting

Now that you are familiar with both knife fighting grips and targets, it's important to make certain that you can maintain the structural integrity of your grip and hold on to your weapon when cutting your adversary.

Unfortunately, I see too many knife fighting instructors place too much emphasis on cutting with the knife and not enough on retention skills.

When I say *retention*, I mean holding on to the knife when delivering a powerful stash or stab. Remember, despite your best efforts to cut soft tissue targets, there's always the good possibility that you'll make contact with something hard and resistant.

Essentially, this means that each and every time you attempt to cut a target, you run the risk of hitting bone and possibly dislodging your knife from your hand. It's just a fact that you have to accept when knife fighting.

Unfortunately, many untrained people have actually dislodged and dropped their knives during a self-defense altercation because they never anticipated the impact shock of their target.

Impact shock is the resistance your hand receives when your knife makes contact with a resistant surface. So, if you want to maintain your grip and hold on to your weapon, you must anticipate this and train for it.

One of the best ways to prepare yourself for impact shock, is to regularly practice slashing and stabbing hard surfaces with your knife. Unfortunately, something like a body opponent bag won't work because its soft material doesn't provide the necessary resistance to truly test the structural integrity of your knife grip.

Don't get me wrong, the body opponent bag is great for knife targeting, but not impact shock training.

Therefore, you will need to find something that provides significant resistance. The best material is wood. Perhaps, a dead tree in your backyard or an old piece of lumber lying around in your garage.

A word of caution, don't slash or stab any hard surfaces with full-force until your grip, hands and arms are first acclimated to the power. My suggestion is to start off with twenty-five percent of your power and progressively increase it over time. And remember to practice all of your knife grips.

Pictured here, a custom-made head target designed specifically for impact shock. It's called the "Bullick" and it's made of locust wood which is extremely hard and will thoroughly test the structural integrity of any knife grip. Be fore-warned, practicing on this type of device will dull the blade of your knife in no time at all. So you might want to consider practicing with a training knife.

Tactical Knife Cuts

Now that you have a solid understanding of knife targeting, it's time to teach you the most efficient and effective ways to acquiring these targets.

As you might imagine, there are several ways to cut your adversary during a knife fight. Some are excellent and some are terrible. For example, some knife cuts include:

- Slash
- Stab
- Flick
- Tear
- Hack
- Butt

For the purposes of practical and effective knife fighting, we only need to focus on two tactical knife cuts; the *slash* and *stab*. Let's take a look at each one.

The Slash

The *slash* is a quick, tight sweeping stroke made with the lower edge of the knife. The slash can be delivered in all three ranges of knife combat and can be perform with either the hammer, saber, ice pick or modified ice pick grips.

Compared to stabs, slashing usually creates a larger surface area wound, so expect things to get bloody very fast!

Whenever executing slashing cuts, avoid wide and long arcing movements. Always keep your "slashing arc" tight and quick by using your wrists and elbows to maneuver the knife. Never lock your elbow

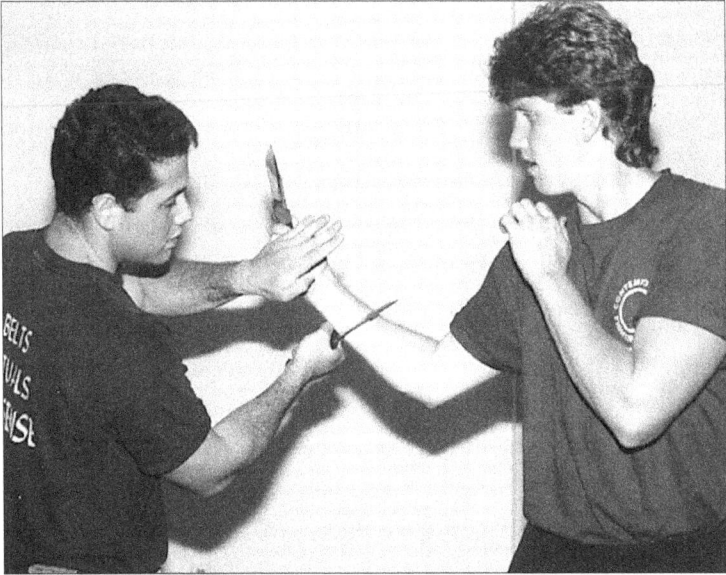

Compared to stabs, slashing usually creates a larger surface area wound, so expect things to get bloody.

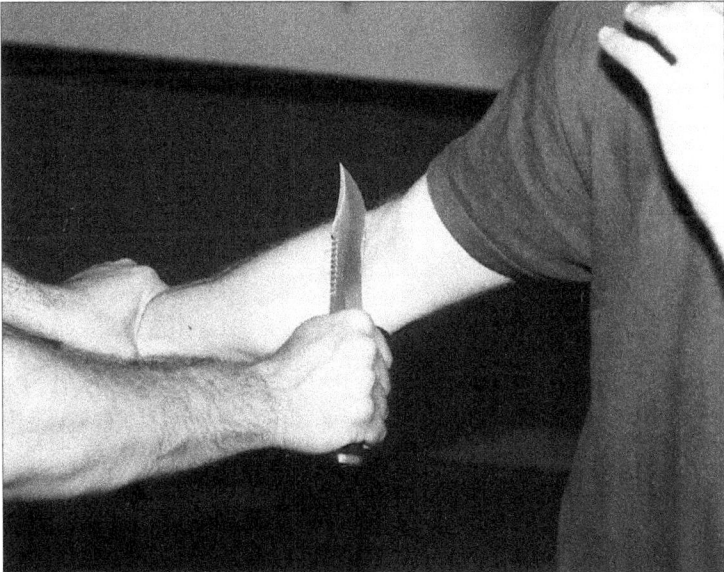

When slashing at your adversary, be certain to make contact with the bottom portion of the blade first and then pull the rest of the blade through the target. This will maximize the size of the wound.

Knife Fighting Targets

when delivering any type of slashing motion. Exaggerated slashing movements are the true mark of a novice and it presents numerous vulnerabilities. Some include: possible elbow dislocation, reduced cutting speed, telegraphic movement, and extreme target exposure.

The contact point of the blade is also very important when performing slashing movements. For example, avoid just making contact with the tip of the blade because this type of flicking movement will do very little to injure or stop your adversary.

When executing the slash, be certain to make contact with the low portion of the blade first (also called the low point of the blade), and then pull the remainder of the knife (mid and high points) through the target. This will create a much deeper cut and produce the greatest amount of damage to the target.

This is when the serrated portion of the blade comes into play during a knife fight. For example, if the serration portion of the blade is located at the lowest point of the blade, you'll be able to penetrate thick protective clothing, allowing the remainder of the blade to make contact with a vital anatomical target.

When slashing, try to direct your blade at a 45-degree angle into the target. This cutting angle is important because it creates a larger arterial wound, and makes it more difficult for arteries to clot when severed at 45-degrees.

Slashing movements are also best delivered to the assailant's arms, eyes, neck, and knee region. Avoid slashing your assailant's torso, which is best suited for stabbing.

BLADE CONTACT POINTS

High portion ➡

Mid portion ➡

Low portion ➡

Successfully delivering a slash during a knife fight requires that you do not forewarn your assailant of your intentions. Clenching your teeth, widening your eyes, cocking knife back, and tensing your neck or shoulders are just a few common telegraphic cues that will negate the element of surprise.

One of the best ways to prevent telegraphic movement is to maintain a poker face prior to executing your attack. Avoid all facial expressions when faced with a threatening assailant. You can study

Knife Fighting Targets

your knife fighting techniques in front of a full-length mirror or have a friend videotape you performing your movements. These procedures will assist you in identifying and ultimately eliminating telegraphic movements. If you are patient and continue to practice, you'll reach your objective.

Finally, you must manage your expectations. Although defeating your adversary with multiple slashes sounds great, it is highly improbable that this can be accomplished under real world knife fighting conditions. The truth is, most assailants will not simply stand there and let you carve them up like a Thanksgiving turkey.

The Stab

The *stab* is a quick and forceful thrust made with the tip of the knife. Stabbing motions puncture body tissue and are more likely to be fatal because it produces severe internal damage and bleeding. You can stab vertically, horizontally and diagonally with either the hammer, saber, ice pick, or modified ice pick grips.

Unlike the slash, the stab can only be utilized in the intermediate and close quarter ranges of knife combat. Never over commit your stab or you will most likely lose your balance and expose vital targets to the assailant.

Novices often make the tragic mistake of jabbing instead of stabbing with their knife. There is a clear difference between jabbing and thrusting a knife. While both movements can puncture your assailant's body, jabbing with a knife is a quick "darting" motion that lacks the necessary force to penetrate the assailant's vital organs.

Jabbing with a knife can also be fatal for some of the following reasons:

1. It clearly informs you adversary that you are fearful of the

encounter and apprehensive to fully engage in the fight. This will most certainly inspire your opponent to attack you with greater conviction and determination.

2. Jabbing wounds are simply ineffective and won't stop a mentally determined knife fighter.

Although the stab requires a 100-percent follow-through and deep penetration into the target, it is generally viewed as the coup de grace - a fully committed killing move.

Finally, when attempting stabs, be exceptionally quick about it. And don't forget that thrusting movements can be delivered at various angles to the assailant's body.

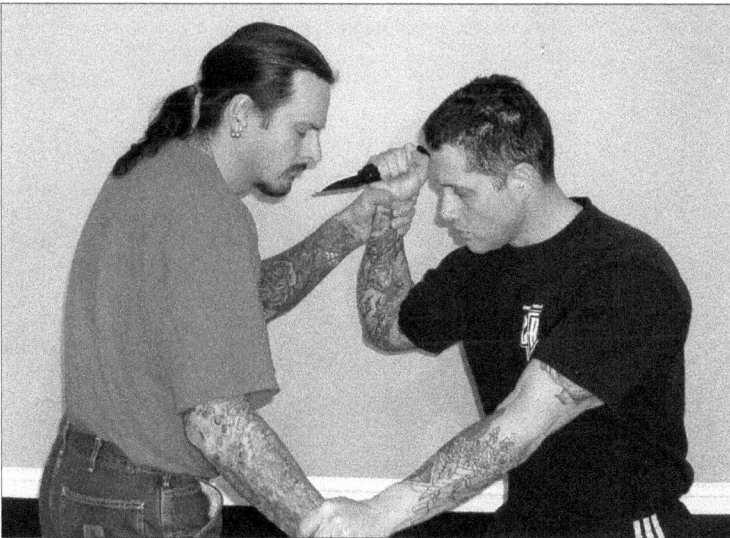

Pictured here, the author (right) delivers a vertical stab.

Here, a diagonal stab or angular thrust.

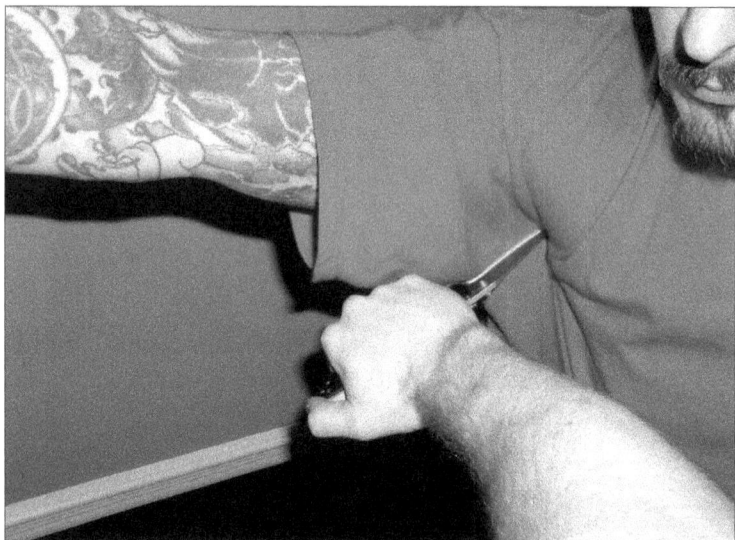

The horizontal stab.

Blade Twisting technique

Blade twisting is used after the blade is plunged into its target. This knife fighting technique is used to increase the size of the wound channel, which will result in faster blood loss and greater structural damage to your assailant.

However, the direction that you twist your blade upon withdrawal is very important and dependent upon the type of thrust that you deliver. For example, when delivering direct stabs with your palm up, turn the knife counterclockwise. When delivering an inward stabs with your palm down, turn your knife clockwise.

Retraction problems when stabbing

Stabbing is not just a matter of thrusting and retracting your knife. You must be aware potential problems that come with stabbing your adversary in a knife fight. More specifically, you must be cognizant of retracting the blade after penetrating your target. Here are a few concerns:

1. Your knife might become extremely slippery from the assailant's blood, making it difficult to positively retract the knife from his body.

2. The suction generates around the wound area of a stab can sometimes make it difficult to withdraw the blade from the assailant's body.

3. Your knife can get lodged between the assailant's bones or joints, making it difficult to retract the blade. For example, knife blades have been known to get lodged into the bones of the ribs.

4. Your knife can get tangled in the assailant's clothes when trying to pull the blade out.

Knife Fighting Targets

To remedy many of these knife retracting problems, use the push-off technique - simply push your assailant away with your free hand as you pull out your blade. This permits a quick withdrawal and throws the assailant off balance, making his counterattack difficult. For maximum power and leverage, apply the push off with your palm up.

The Nine Angle Numbering System

Just about every knife fighting system will have their own unique numbering system. Some are very basic while others are unnecessarily complex. In fact, there are some knife fighting systems that have over forty different attack angles.

If you are truly concerned about surviving a knife fight (as I hope you are), you'll want to steer clear of such complex numbering system and use something that is simple, practical and easy to remember under the extreme duress of a deadly knife fight.

Over the past thirty years, I have designed a *nine angle numbering system* that is efficient, effective, and safe for both offensive and defensive knife fighting applications.

Moreover, this numbering system seamlessly integrates with all of the tactical knife grips (hammer, saber, icepick and modified ice pick) providing the user with an instantaneous slashing and stabbing delivery system. Let's take a closer look at each angle of attack. We will start with angle 1.

Angle 1

Angle One is a diagonal slash or stab traveling from right to left. Targets can include your assailant's ear canal, back of neck, carotid artery, subclavian artery, throat, brachial, radial or ulnar arteries, triceps, femoral artery, back of knee, and wrist flexor.

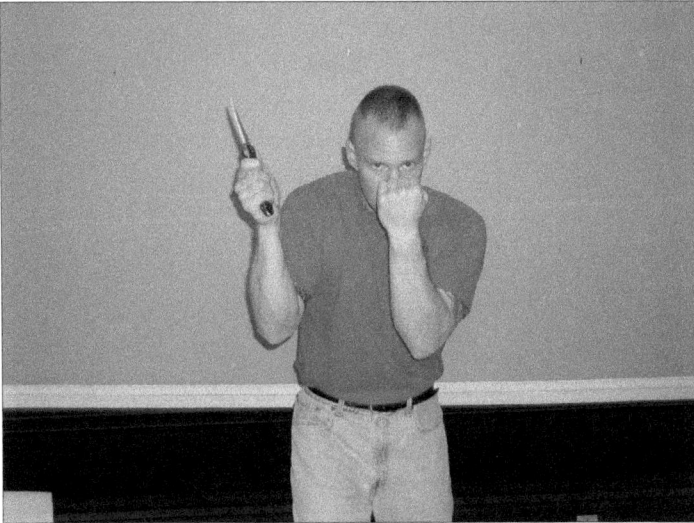

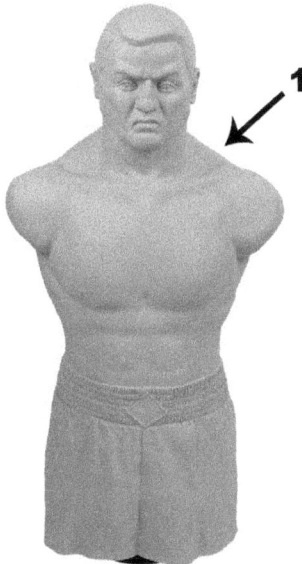

Angle 2

Angle Two is a diagonal slash or stab traveling from left to right. Targets can include your assailant's ear canal, back of neck, carotid artery, subclavian artery, throat, brachial, radial or ulnar arteries, triceps, femoral artery, back of knee, and wrist flexor.

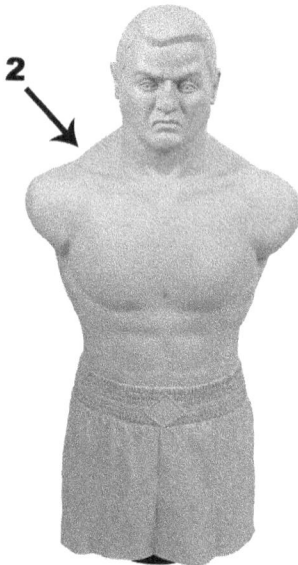

Angle 3

Angle Three is a horizontal slash or stab traveling from right to left. Targets can include your assailant's ear canal, lateral side of the head, back of neck, carotid artery, throat, brachial, radial and ulnar arteries, triceps, femoral artery, back of knee, and wrist flexor.

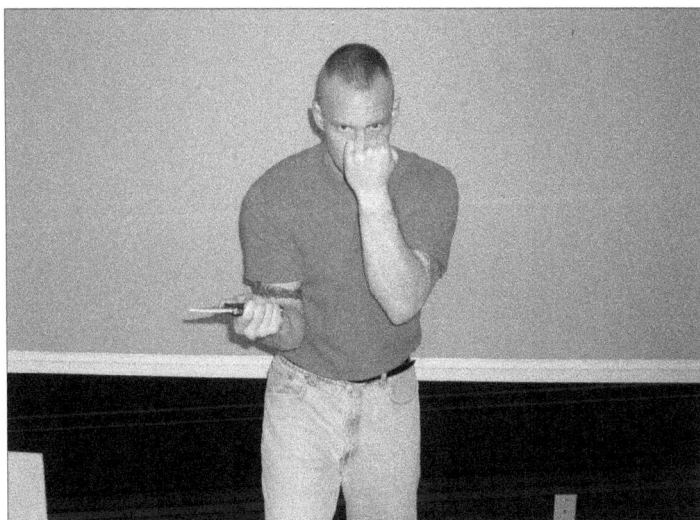

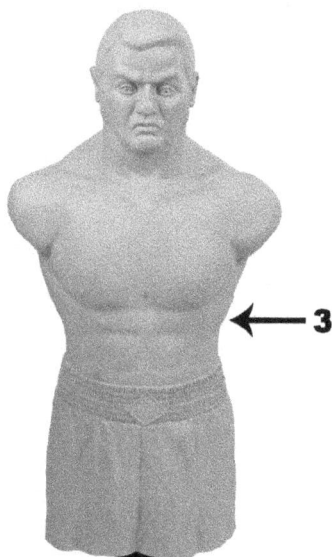

Angle 4

Angle Four is a horizontal slash or stab traveling from left to right. Targets can include your assailant's ear canal, lateral side of the head, back of neck, carotid artery, throat, brachial, radial and ulnar arteries, triceps, femoral artery, back of knee, and wrist flexor.

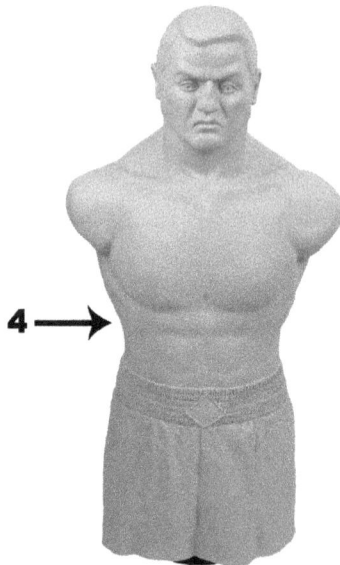

Angle 5

Angle Five is an upward diagonal slash or stab moving from right to left. Targets can include your assailant's carotid artery, axillary artery, brachial, radial or ulnar arteries, triceps, femoral artery, back of knee, and wrist flexor.

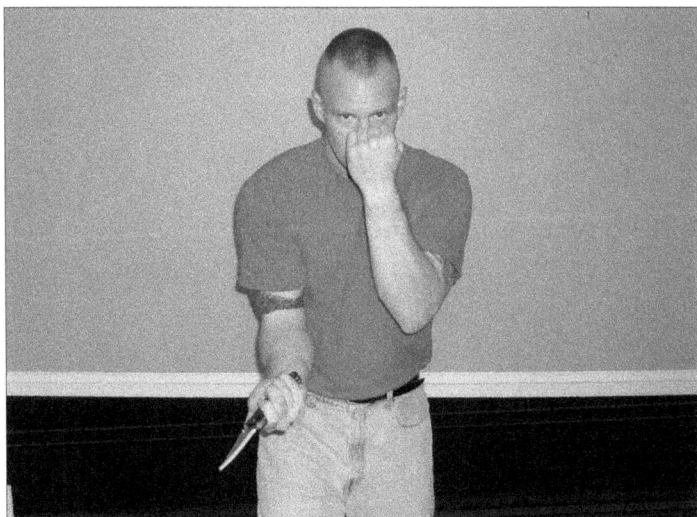

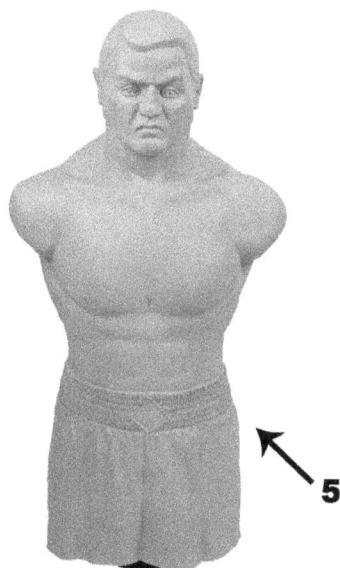

Angle 6

Angle Six is an upward diagonal slash or stab moving from left to right. Targets can include your assailant's carotid artery, axillary artery, brachial, radial or ulnar arteries, triceps, femoral artery, back of knee, and wrist flexor.

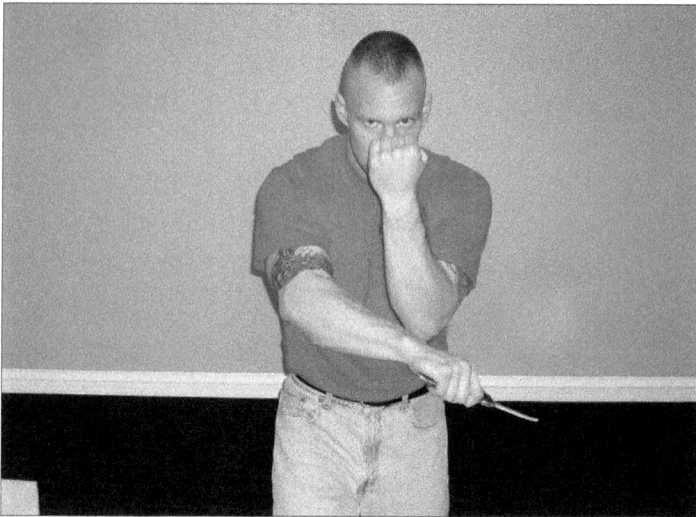

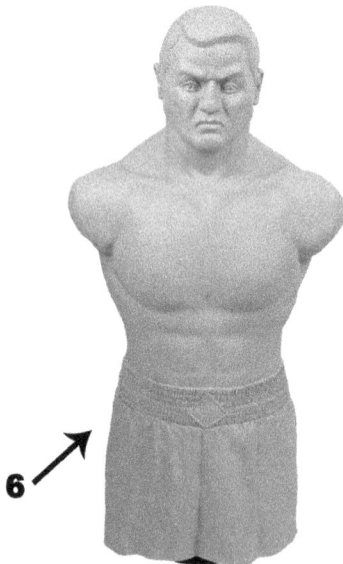

Angle 7

Angle Seven is a linear stab. Anatomical targets include the assailant's eyes, ear canal, lateral side of the head, throat, heart, back of neck, and groin.

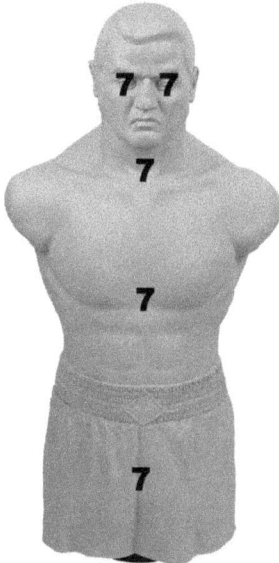

Angle 8

Angle Eight is a downward vertical slash or stab. Targets can include your assailant's eyes, back of neck, carotid artery, subclavian artery, throat, brachial, radial or ulnar arteries, triceps, femoral artery, back of knee, and wrist flexor.

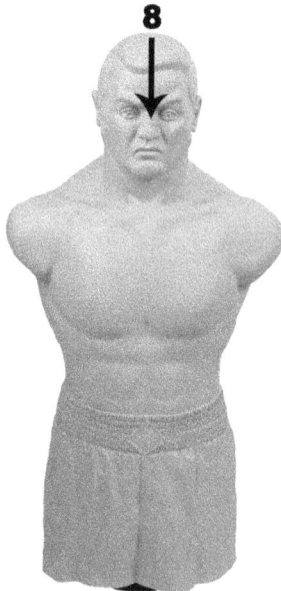

Angle 9

Angle Nine is an upward vertical slash or stab. Targets can include your assailant's throat, heart, carotid artery, axillary artery, brachial, radial or ulnar arteries, triceps, femoral artery, groin, back of knee, and wrist flexor.

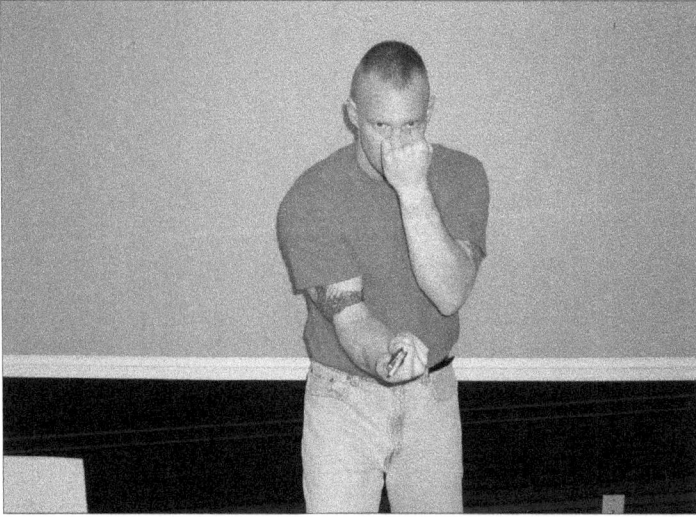

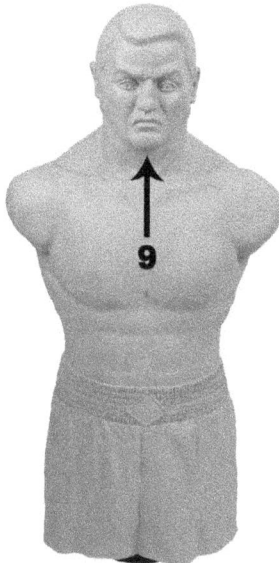

The Nine Angles of Attack

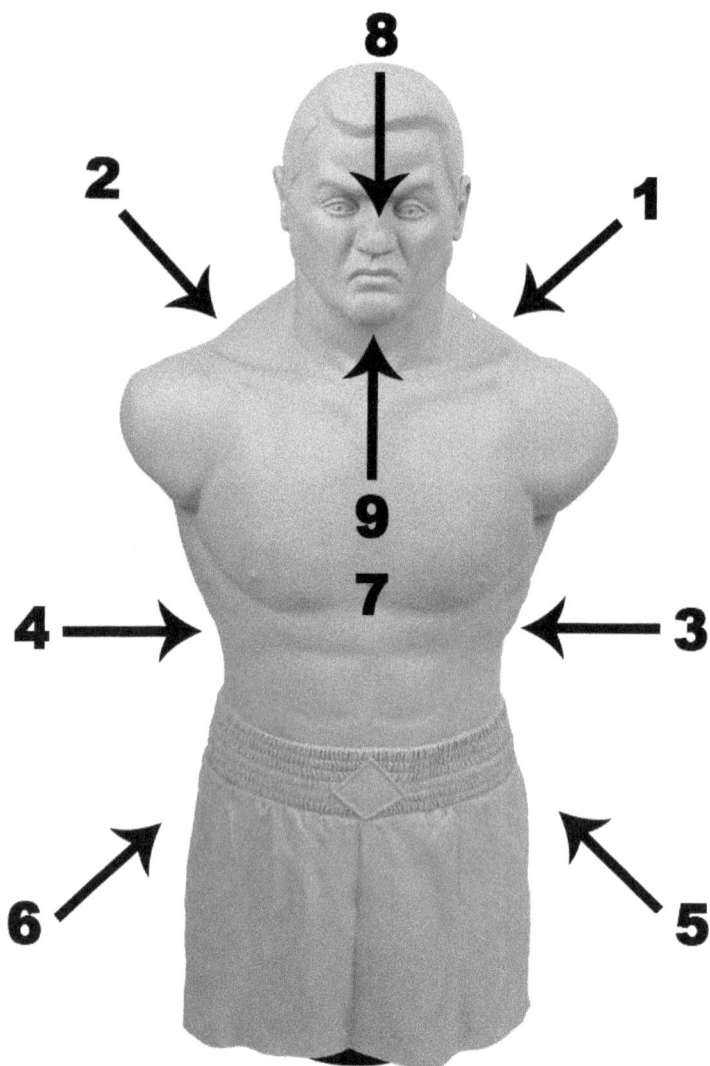

Power Cuts and the Body Box

Power is one of the most overrated attributes of tactical knife fighting. In fact, if your blade is sharp enough, you really won't need a lot of power to penetrate a fleshy anatomical target.

Beginners often make the tragic mistake of power cutting, which often requires their knife to travel 180-degrees across their body. Not only does this slow down a cutting combination, it also leaves you vulnerable to a swift counterattack.

Therefore, it's important for you to always keep your cuts tight and close to your body. During both offensive and defensive techniques, you must also be mindful of your cutting force and make certain the cuts stays within your *body box*.

When performing both offensive and defensive cutting movements, you must always make a concerted effort to keep you cuts within your body box. Pictured here, the boundaries of your body box.

Three Phases of a Knife Cut

To better understand the inherent vulnerability of a power cut, we can divide a knife cut into three phases. They are:

1. **Initiation phase** - the starting point of your cut.

2. **Mid phase** - the contact point of your cut, where your blade makes contact with its target.

3. **Completion phase** - the end point of your cut.

Again, its critical that all three phases of you knife cut are performed within your body box.

Tactical knife fighting requires that you keep your cuts very tight and close to your body. Here, a student demonstrates the dangerous vulnerability of a power cut. Notice how the completion phase of his cut is outside his body box.

Combination Cutting

Most unarmed combat situations will require more than just a single strike to stop your attacker. In fact, you will almost always have to initiate a strategic compound attack. This also applies to tactical knife fighting.

A combination attack is what immediately follows your initial cut, and it's defined as the logical sequence of two or more cuts strategically thrown in succession. The objective is to take the fight out of the assailant and the assailant out of the knife fight by destroying his defenses with a burst of full-speed cuts.

Based on speed, timing, target selection, and target exploitation, the compound attack also requires calculation, precision, and clarity. To maximize your compound attack, you must have a thorough knowledge and awareness of the knife targets presented by your adversary. Remember, unless your assailant is in full body armor, there are always targets. It is simply a question of your selecting them and attacking quickly with the appropriate cuts.

Cutting Combination Examples
Combination One: Angle 1- Angle 2 - Angle 7

Step 1: Begin with the angle 1 cut.

Step 2: Next, angle 2.

Step 3: Follow up with the angle 7 stab.

Combination Two: Angle 1- Angle 2 - Angle 3 - Angle 4

Step 1: Begin with angle 1.

Step 2: Next, angle 2.

Step 3: Follow up with angle 3.

Step 4: Finish with the angle 4 slash.

Combination Three: Angle 7- Angle 8 - Angle 9

Step 1: Begin with the angle 7 stab.

Step 2: Next, attack with angle 8.

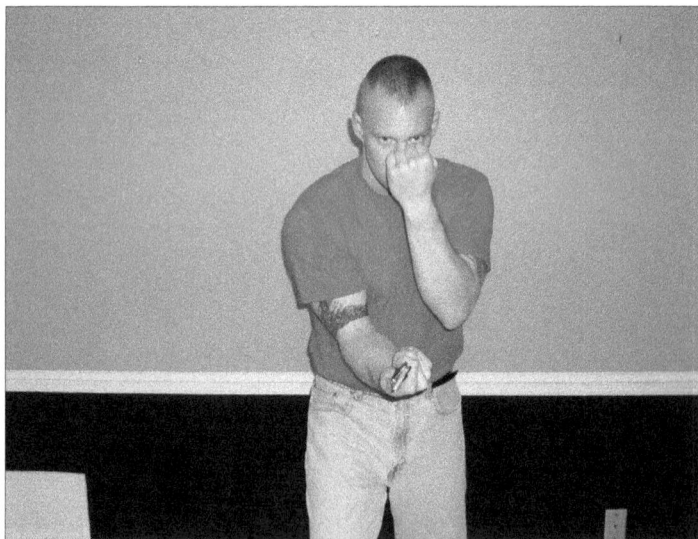

Step 3: Finish with angle 9.

Combination Four: Angle 3- Angle 4 - Angle 3 - Angle 4

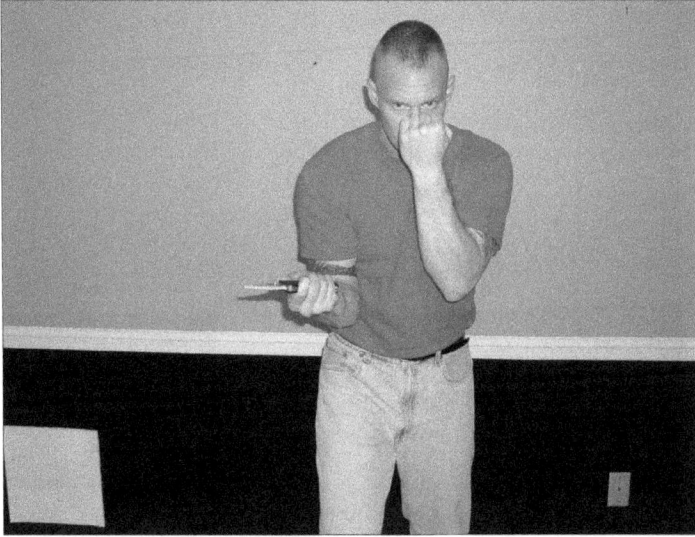

Step 1: Begin with angle 3.

Step 2: Next, angle 4.

Step 3: Quickly follow with another angle 3.

Step 4: Finish with angle 4.

Combination Five: Angle 1- Angle 2 - Angle 5 - Angle 6

Step 1: Begin with angle 1.

Step 2: Next, angle 2.

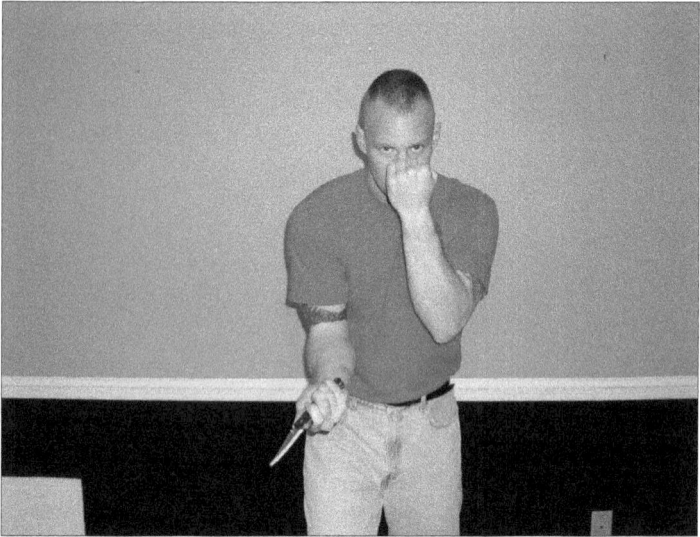

Step 3: Follow up with angle 5.

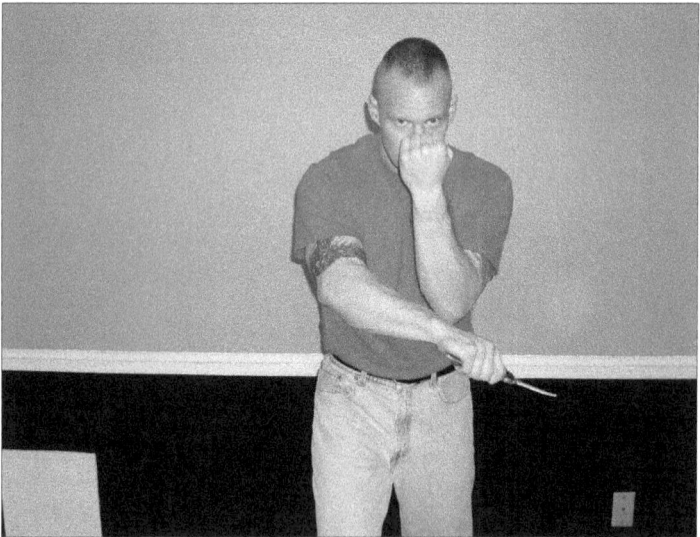

Step 4: Finish with angle 6.

Combination Six: Angle 8- Angle 9 - Angle 8 - Angle 9

Step 1: Start with angle 8.

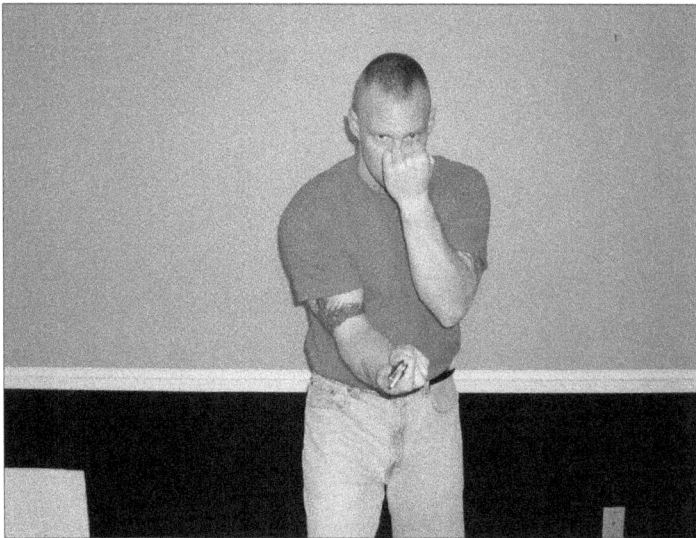

Step 2: Next, angle 9.

Step 3: Follow up with another angle 8.

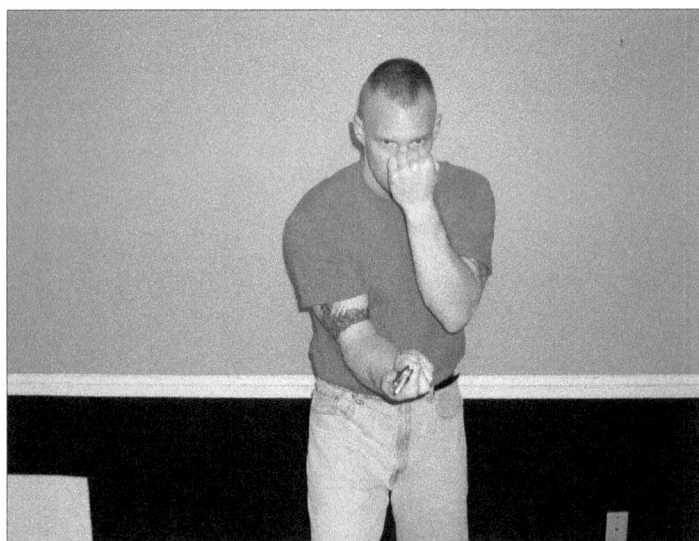

Step 4: Finish with angle 9.

Combination Seven: Angle 7- Angle 7 - Angle 9 - Angle 4

Step 1: Begin with angle 7 stab.

Step 2: Quickly retract your arms back and deliver another angle 7.

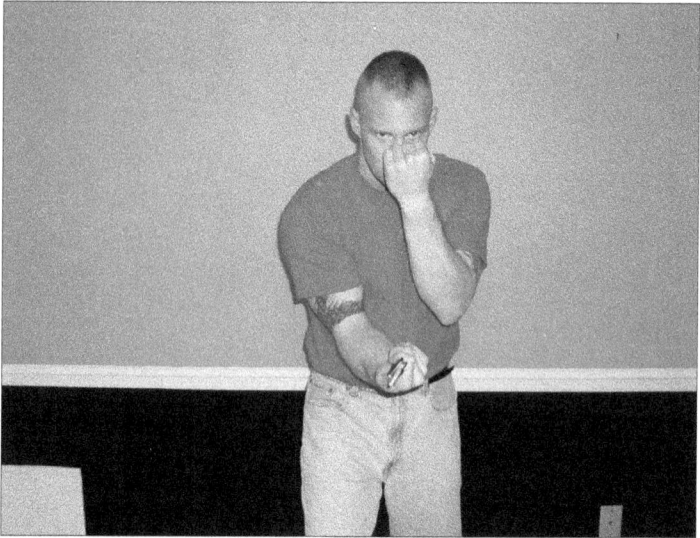

Step 3: Next, angle 9.

Step 4: Finish with angle 4.

Combination Eight: Angle 5- Angle 6 - Angle 3 - Angle 4 - Angle 9

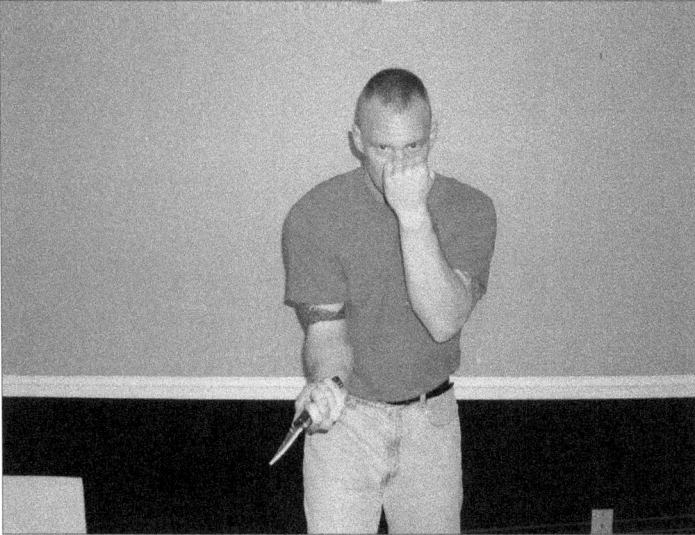

Step 1: Start with angle 5.

Step 2: Next, angle 6.

Step 3: Follow up with angle 3.

Step 4: Deliver angle 4.

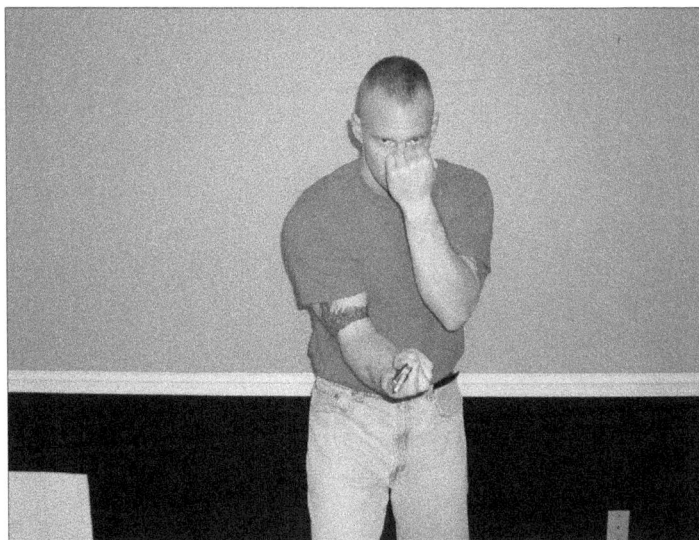

Step 5: Finish with the angle 9.

Combination Nine: Angle 1- Angle 6 - Angle 5 - Angle 2 - Angle 7

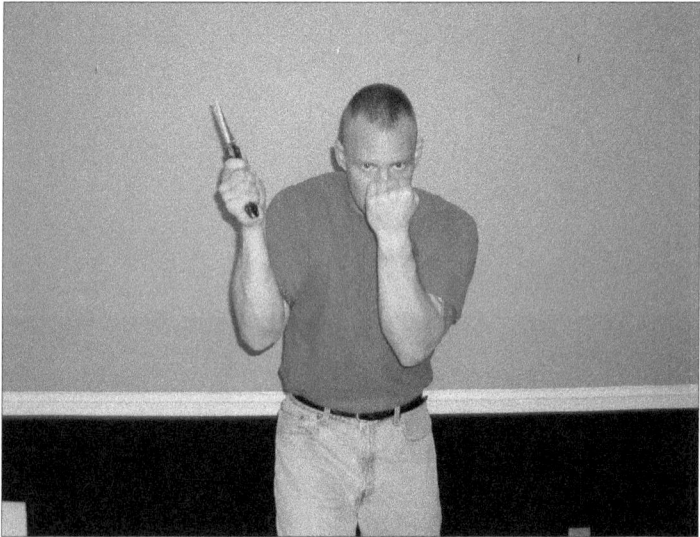

Step 1: Begin with angle 1.

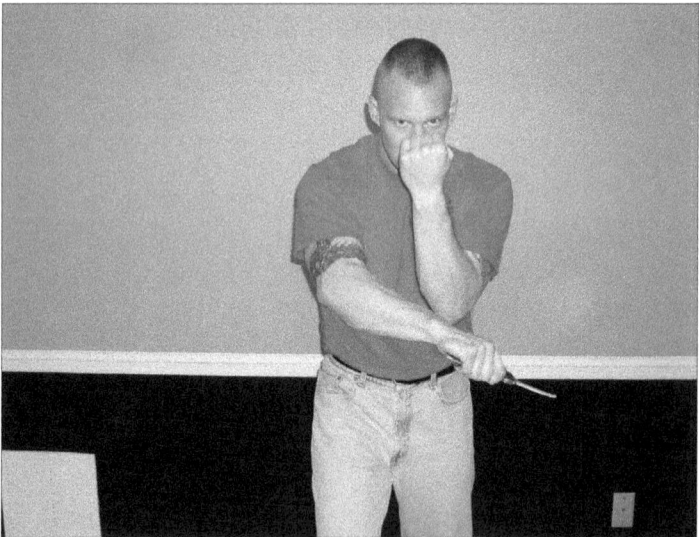

Step 2: Next, angle 6.

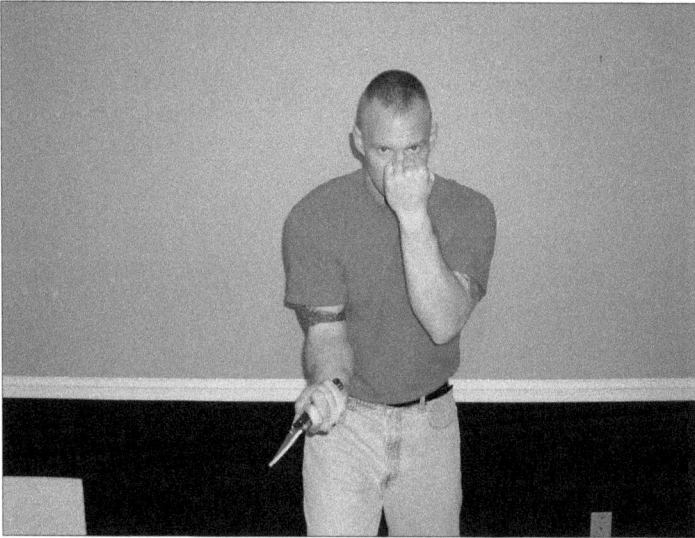

Step 3: Follow with angle 5.

Step 4: Deliver angle 2.

Knife Fighting Targets

Step 5: Finish with the angle 7 stab.

Combination Ten: Angles 1 through 9

Step 1: Begin with the angle 1.

Step 2: Next, angle 2.

Step 3: Follow with angle 3.

Step 4: Deliver angle 4.

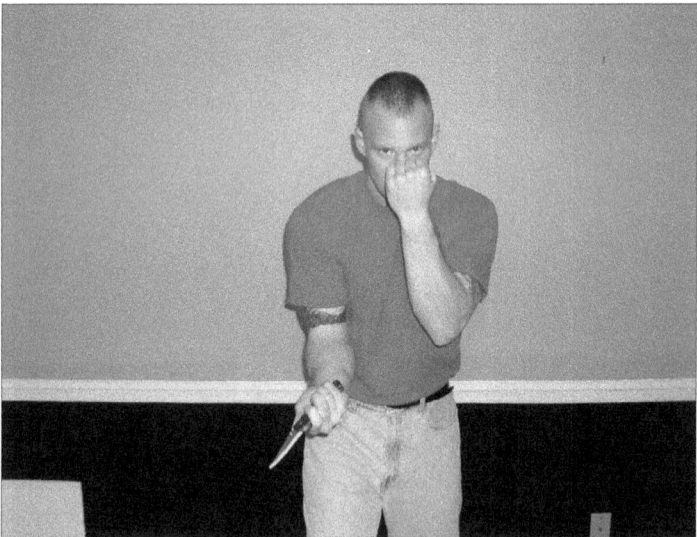

Step 5: Follow up with the angle 5 cut.

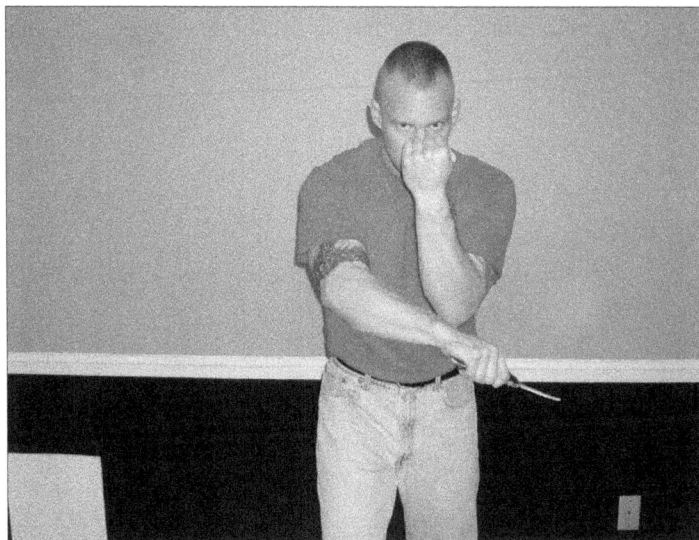

Step 6: Angle 6.

Step 7: Execute angle 7.

Step 8: Follow up with angle 8.

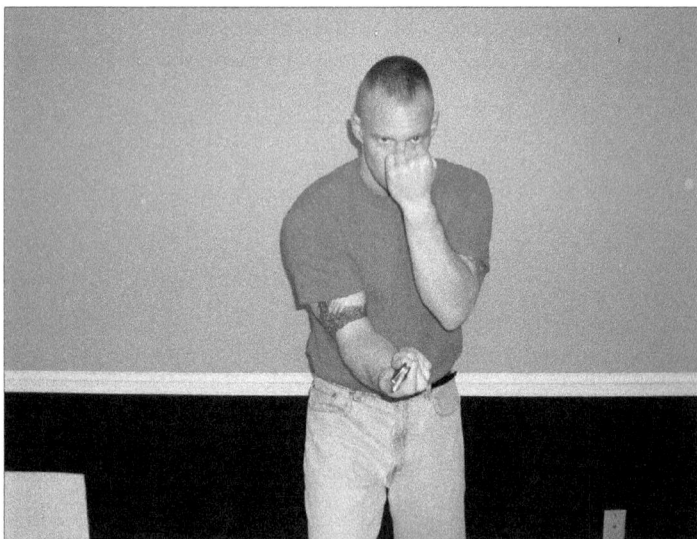

Step 9: Finish with the angle 9.

Creating Your Own Knife Fighting Combinations

As you can imagine, there are an infinite amount of cutting combinations you can practice. To help get you started, I've provided a section for you to write some of them down.

1.

2.

3.

4.

5.

6.

7.

8.

9.

Knife Fighting Targets

10.

11.

12.

13.

14.

15.

16.

17.

18.

19.

20.

Cuts must be fast and fluid

When you proceed with the compound attack, always maintain the offensive flow. The offensive flow is a progression of continuous offensive movements designed to neutralize your adversary.

The key is to have each cut flow smoothly and efficiently from one to the next without causing you to lose ground. Subjecting your adversary to an offensive flow is especially effective because it taxes his nervous system, thereby dramatically lengthening his defensive reaction time.

In a knife fight it's critical that you always keep the offensive pressure on until your opponent is completely neutralized. Always remember that letting your offensive flow stagnate, even for a second, will open you up to numerous dangers and risks.

Proper breathing is another substantial element of the compound attack, and there is one simple rule that should be followed: exhale during the execution phase of your cut and inhale during its completion phase. Above all, never hold your breath when delivering several consecutive cuts. Doing so could lead to dizziness and fainting, among other complications.

You Don't Have Much Time

Your body can only sustain delivering a compound attack for so long. Initially, your brain will quickly release adrenaline into your blood stream, which will fuel your fighting and enhance your strength and power. This lethal boost of energy is known as an adrenaline dump. However, your ability to exert and maintain this maximum effort will last no more than 30 to 60 seconds if you are in above-average shape. If the fight continues after that, your strength and speed may drop by as much as 50 percent below normal. When all is said and done, you don't have much time in a knife fight, so the battle needs to be won fast before your energy runs out!

Don't Forget To Relocate!

Subsequent to your compound attack, immediately move to a new location by flanking your adversary. This tactic is known as relocating. Based on the principles of strategy, movement, and surprise, relocating dramatically enhances your safety by making it difficult for your adversary to identify your position after you have cut him. Remember, if your opponent doesn't know exactly where you are, he won't be able to effectively counterattack.

Actuate Recovery Breathing

Breathing is one of the most important and often neglected aspects of knife fighting. Proper breathing promotes muscular relaxation and increases the speed and efficiency of your cuts. The rate at which you breathe will also determine how quickly your body can recover from a violent encounter.

Implementing an explosive compound attack with a knife will often leave you winded. Because of the volatile nature of knife fight, even highly conditioned fighters will show signs of oxygen debt. Hence it's important to employ recovery breathing, the active process of quickly restoring your breathing to its normal state. It requires taking long, deep breaths in a controlled rhythm while avoiding rapid, short gasping. Wind sprints are great for improving your recovery breathing. Consider adding them to your knife training program.

Understanding knife wound reaction dynamics

In my book, *Maximum Damage: Hidden Secrets Behind Brutal Fighting Combinations*, I define *probable reaction dynamics* (PRD) as the opponent's anticipated movements or actions that occur in both armed and unarmed combat. Probable reaction dynamics will always be the result or residual of your initial cut with a knife.

The most basic example of probable reaction dynamics during a knife fight can be illustrated by the following scenario. For example, your adversary attempts to cut you and you immediately counter cut him with a deep slash to his wrist flexor. When your blade comes in contact with its target, your opponent will exhibit one of several "possible" physical or psychological reactions to your cut. These responses might include:

- The opponent reflexively retracts his injured arm.
- The opponent grabs or covers his wound.
- The opponent frantically looks for an escape route.
- The opponent continually looks at his injured wrist.
- The opponent goes into shock.

Knowledge of your assailant's probable reaction dynamics is vital during a knife fight. In fact, you must be mindful of the possible reaction dynamics to every possible angle of attack. This is what I refer to as "reaction dynamic awareness" and I can assure you this is not such an easy task. However, with proper training and analysis, it can be developed.

Regardless of your knife fighting style, understanding and ultimately mastering reaction dynamic awareness will give you a tremendous advantage by maximizing the effectiveness, efficiency, and safety of your knife fighting skills.

Probable Reaction Dynamic Exercise

Write down the different probable reaction dynamics to the following knife wounds. Don't forget to include both your opponent's offensive and defensive reactions.

A slash to the inside forearm:

1.

2.

3.

4.

5.

A slash to the biceps:

1.

2.

3.

4.

5.

A slash to the inner thigh (femoral artery):

1.

2.

3.

4.

5.

A slash to the back of the knee:

1.

2.

3.

4.

5.

A stab under the armpit:

1.

2.

3.

4.

5.

A stab to the groin:

1.

2.

3.

4.

5.

Knife Fighting Targets

Chapter 4
Knife Fighting Battle Plan

Knife Fighting Targets

Your knife fighting blueprint

Knife targeting is not enough to survive a knife fight. You'll need a battle plan or blueprint that will help guide you through the chaos of edged weapon combat.

The following blueprint is simple yet practical and it includes all of the critical knife fighting strategies you will need to survive the encounter and get you home alive and in one piece. Let's begin with the critical importance of distancing.

Make some distance

If you have the chance to run and escape prior to or during a knife fight, do it *immediately*! Quickly try to scan your environment for possible escape routes. Your goal at this point is to stay as far away from assailant's knife as possible.

Look for doors, windows, stairwells, or other avenues of safe escape. Under no circumstances should you engage in a knife fight unless it is absolutely necessary. Don't let your ego or pride trap you into believing that it's cowardly to run from a knife fight. However, if you attempt to outrun your adversary, be certain that you have the athletic ability to really move - and don't offer him target opportunities in your flight.

At the same time, if your situation permits, *allow your assailant an avenue of escape*. Most reasonable people will choose to run instead of tangle with another knife fighter. Avoid making the tragic mistake of forcing your assailant into a corner.

Bring attention to your situation

Try to attract attention to your situation by screaming out loud to anyone who will listen. For example, a nearby witness itching to video the encounter on his or her smartphone might be just enough of a deterrence to your adversary.

Verbally discourage your adversary

Finally, if there's time, try to reason with your adversary and discourage him to engage in the knife fight. Remind him of the inherent dangerous consequences (i.e., maiming, disfigurement, death, jail time, etc) of your fateful encounter.

Remember, you must do *everything* in your power to avoid this deadly encounter. However, a word of caution. If your adversary is mentally deranged or high on drugs, there's a very good possibility your words will be ignored.

Cut the knife out of his hand

Something as simple as an avenue of escape can make all the difference between life and death for both you and your adversary.

If the knife fight in absolutely unavoidable, you must approach it offensively and attack first! Don't wait for your adversary to make the first move. Just like my first strike principle, you must cut first, cut fast, cut with authority, and keep the pressure on until the threat is stopped.

Assuming your adversary isn't fighting you from a rear hand knife stance, your primary objective is to cut his knife hand. From a knife fighting stance, attack his hand or wrist (the one holding the blade of course) with quick, penetrating slashes.

In the event your adversary confronts you with a rear hand knife stance, apply the *CWCT* (closest weapon to closes target) principle by cutting his lead hand and arm to pieces.

Again, if you successfully manage to cut or injure the opponent, immediately discourage him from continuing the fight, encourage him to flee from the encounter. If he's somewhat reasonable, he might just do so.

Continue to scan for escape routes

If your adversary refuses to flee from the fight, despite his injury, see if any escape routes have opened up for you. In fact, throughout the knife fighting encounter, you should continue to scan the environment for opportunities to safely escape from the fight. Just don't get distracted, remember you are engaged in a deadly knife fight and need to focus on your immediate threat.

If necessary, escalate target classification

Depending on how your opponent reacts to your initial hand immobilizer attack, you might have to escalate your attack to either a bleeder or quick kill target. This, however, will require you to employ the combination cutting principle that was discussed in the previous chapter.

Remember to constantly assess your opponent's mental and physical condition during the encounter. For example, some opponents might flee from the encounter when they catch sight of their own blood. But there are others who, despite their injuries, will become even more determined to go after you. The bottom line is there are no absolutes and every knife fighting encounter should be approached on a case-by-case basis.

Keep both you and your knife moving

Once the actual fight begins, try to keep both you and your knife moving. This is important for the following reasons:

1. It prevents inertia from setting in and slowing you down.

2. Movement enhances the overall velocity of your cuts.

3. It helps minimizes telegraphing prior to cutting.

4. It enhances your defensive reaction time.

5. It minimizes your hand and digit exposure in the event your attacker wants to counterattack your hands.

6. It significantly enhances your offensive flow during the course of your cutting combination.

7. It helps your assailant misjudge your weapon's range.

Expect to get cut during the encounter

Whether you're unarmed and defending against a knife attack or knife fighting with your adversary, expect to get cut. This frame of mind is critical for the following reasons:

1. It prepares you for the cold reality of edged-weapon combat.

2. It helps prevent you from going into mental shock if you do get cut.

3. It frees you from the immediate fear, worry, and mental concern of your well-being.

Ignore your wound

If you do get cut, do not look at your wound. You must ignore it until the threat is eliminated. Actually, looking at your wound in the middle of a knife fight can be dangerous for the following four reasons:

1. It takes your eyes off of your immediate threat - the assailant and his knife.

2. It can psyche you out.

3. It may cause you to go into shock.

4. It will immediately empower your assailant.

Knife Quick Draw Skills

How you draw your knife is a personal decision that is largely dependent upon some of the following factors:

- Where you carry your knife.

- The size and weight of your knife.

- The type of knife (tactical folder or fixed blade).

- Weapon concealment laws in your area.

However, the most important factor that determines the quick draw speed of your knife is *where* you carry your weapon. For example, will you be carrying your knife in your front pants pocket, on your belt, in your boot, a shoulder harness, a necklace sheath, EDC bag, etc.

The next important consideration will be the actual knife drawing technique. There are two types:

- **Same side draw** - you carry and draw your knife on the same side of your body.

- **Cross draw** - your hand will "cross over" your body to draw your knife.

Personally, I prefer the same side draw technique because, unlike the cross draw method, you don't run the possible risk of having your adversary trap your hand or arm when it crosses your body. My motto has always been, keep it simple and safe!

Quick Draw Mirror Drill

Regardless of the drawing style you use, you'll want to practice until your technique is quick, smooth, and non telegraphic. Training in front of a mirror is one of the best ways to improve your knife drawing speed.

1. Begin by standing in front of a full-length mirror with both

of your hands relaxed and down at your sides.

2. Next, without looking at your knife, quickly draw your weapon while simultaneously assuming a solid knife fighting stance.

3. When you assume your stance, scrutinize yourself and pick out the strategic deficiencies. For example, are you holding your knife in the proper grip? Are any of your targets exposed? Is your balance sacrificed? Are your knees bent? Is your knife close to your body?

4. Perform this exercise for three to five minutes and then take a two-minute break. Begin again for another three to five minutes.

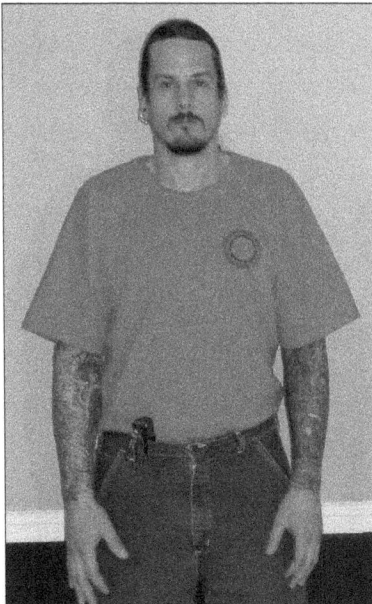

Begin the quick draw mirror drill with both of your hands down by your sides. Note: The knife is intentionally left in a high seated position so the reader can see the exact location of the weapon.

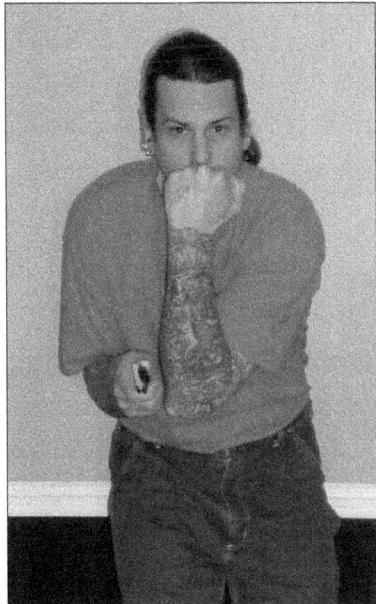

Next, without looking at your knife, quickly draw your weapon while simultaneously assuming a solid knife fighting stance.

What about defensive knife fighting?

If you're familiar with my work, then you'll know that I don't pull punches. This is especially true when it comes to the lethal world of knife fighting.

So, I'll cut to the chase and get to the point (no pun intended). Defensive knife fighting is a dangerous concept perpetuated by well-meaning instructors who don't have the slightest clue about the real horrors of edged weapon combat.

First, a defensive knife fighter is one who permits his adversary to seize and maintain offensive control in a fight. Beware! This defensive mind-set can get you killed. Simply put, allowing your antagonist the opportunity to deliver the first cut is tactical suicide. It's like allowing a gunslinger to draw his pistol first.

Never forget that if you permit the adversary to cut first, he might injure or possibly kill you, and he will most certainly force you into an irreversible defensive flow that can preclude you from issuing an effective counterattack with your weapon.

As I said earlier, knife fighting is fast, furious and often fatal. It's not like anything you've see on television or in the movies. It truly is a horrific event that any sane person would not want to experience.

Consider this scenario: imagine you are forced into a knife fight with a mentally deranged knife attacker who is fueled by adrenaline, rage, and fear. His attacks will blind, frenzied flurry of slashes and stabs. To make matters worse, he also might be amped up on psychoactive drugs like amphetamines, cocaine, and PCP. This is a type of adversary who has absolutely *nothing to lose!*

Even the most well-trained knife fighter will have his work cut out for him when dealing with an unskilled and enraged madman armed with a knife. A crazed knife attack is simply to unpredictable and frenetic to manage with conventional defensive knife fighting techniques. The nature and unpolished characteristics of a crazed knife attacker will often be too overwhelming to counter effectively.

Therefore, whenever you are engaged in a knife fight and there is no way to diffuse the situation or escape safely, you must cut first. This offensive strategy is known as my first-strike principle, and it's essential to the process of neutralizing a formidable adversary in a knife encounter.

One inescapable fact about knife fighting is the longer the encounter lasts, the greater your chances of serious injury or even death. Common sense suggests that you must end the encounter as quickly as possible.

Cutting first is the best method of achieving this tactical objective because it permits you to neutralize your assailant swiftly while, at the same time, precluding his ability to retaliate effectively. No time is wasted, and no unnecessary risks are taken.

When it comes to reality based knife fighting, the element of surprise is invaluable. Delivering the first cut gives you the upper hand because it allows you to injure the criminal adversary suddenly and unexpectedly.

Employing the first cut principle requires an offensive mentality that compels you to act rather than react. You must be aggressive and take affirmative and absolute control of the situation by making all the decisions and acting immediately without apprehension or trepidation.

Unfortunately, some knife fighting instructors teach their students to wait for their opponent to make the first move. Big mistake! In the world of edged weapon combat, this reactive type of approach will get you a one-way trip to the city morgue.

There are also knife fighting practitioners who are simply too timid to take the initiative and cut first. Many won't cut first because they simply lack the confidence to do so. Others are uncertain about the legal requirements and justifications, and, as a result, they second-guess their instincts, hesitate, and end up injured or dead.

Let me be clear, defensive knife fighting techniques are not a complete waste of time. In fact, they can be very useful and can ultimately save your life if the circumstances are right. My point is, don't approaching a knife fight defensively. Instead, approach it offensively and your odds of surviving the encounter will increase exponentially.

Defensive knife fighting techniques can be very useful and can ultimately save your life if the circumstances are right.

Defensive Techniques

While offensive knife fighting techniques are your bread and butter, there might be the need to apply defensive maneuvers. There are three staple defensive knife fighting techniques you should add to your repertoire. I often refer to them as counter cutting moves and they include the Meet, Pass and Follow. Let's take a look at each one.

The Meet Technique

The *Meet* is a defensive knife fighting technique applied in both the mid and close-quarter knife ranges. Its primary function is to intercept your assailant's line of attack with a slash to his wrist. Since you are still positioned within your assailant's line of attack, be certain to use a safety check to prevent the assailant's knife from following through.

Once the open hand safety check is applied, you must grab the assailant's wrist to temporarily prevent further use of his weapon.

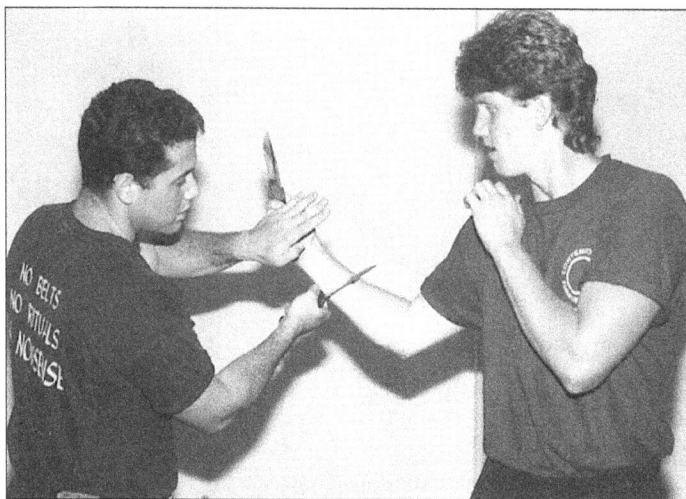

When applying the meet, be certain to use an open hand safety check to prevent the assailant's knife from following through.

The Pass Technique

The *Pass* is another defensive technique that can be executed in the mid and long knife ranges. Like the meet, the function of the pass is to intercept your assailant's line of attack with a cut to his wrist. When employing this defensive maneuver, be certain to lean back and angle your torso away from your assailant's strike. Generally, when employing the pass (at long knife range), there is no need for a safety check.

Here, the author (left) demonstrates the pass technique.

The Follow Technique

The third and final defensive technique is called the *Follow* and it's used in the mid to long distance of knife combat. Like the pass, the follow requires you to lean back and angle your torso away from your assailant's strike. However, instead of cutting your adversary's wrist, you would execute a backhand cut to his hand or wrist. In essence, you are "following" after your assailant's line of attack.

Pictured here, the follow technique.

Counter Cut and Control

The primary objective with defensive knife fighting is to counter cut the opponent's knife hand and gain control of it with a powerful wrist grab. Failure to do so will only prolong the encounter and offer the adversary the opportunity to continue his knife assault. Remember, grabbing the assailant's wrist is the only way to gain control of his weapon during a knife fight.

As I discussed earlier, the safety check is a critical component of this defensive strategy for the following two reasons:

1. It momentarily prevents the assailant's knife from following through with it's cut path.

2. Once the safety check is executed, it instantly turns into a wrist grab.

Pictured here, the practitioner on the left demonstrates a safety check which momentarily prevents the assailant's knife from following through with it's cut path.

Here, the practitioner turns his safety check into a wrist grab.

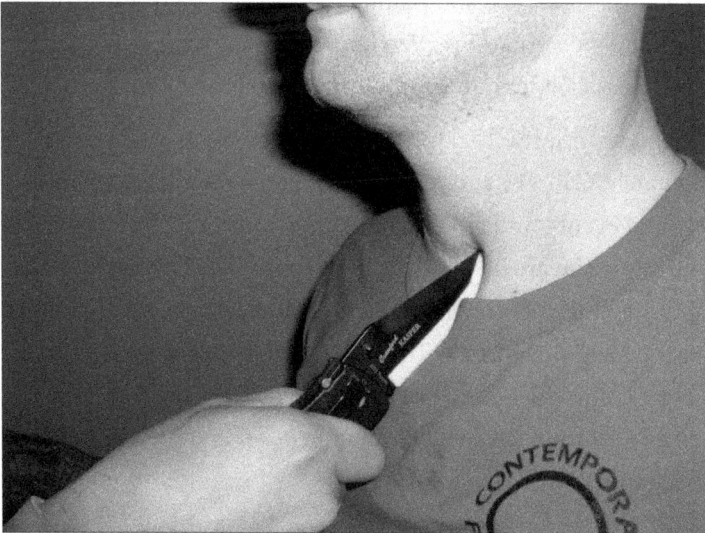

Once the weapon hand is controlled, the practitioner can deliver a more lethal cut.

The Aftermath of a Knife Fight

One important and often neglected aspect of knife fighting is dealing with the aftermath of the encounter. Many people don't realize that the aftermath of deadly violence often carries many physical, psychological, and legal ramifications. What do you do after a confrontation with a knife wielding assailant? Do you know what to prepare for? Whom to talk to? Where to get help? The following principles and tips will answer these important questions and ultimately prepare you for the aftermath of a knife fight.

Emergency first aid & medical attention

Once the confrontation is over and there is no apparent danger, conduct an immediate inventory of your body. Quickly scan your torso, hands, arms, legs, and feet for any signs of cuts. Run your hands down your face and over your head and neck to check for blood. For those of you who might think it's silly and unnecessary to check yourself, think again. Many times people are seriously injured after a knife fight and don't even know it because the adrenaline rush from the flight-or-flight response shuts off pain.

If you are injured, seek professional medical assistance immediately. Call 911 and request an ambulance. Stay calm, breathe slowly and evenly, and tell the dispatcher your exact location. In the meantime, if you are bleeding heavily, apply direct pressure to the wound site. If the wound is located in a limb, elevate the extremity above the level of the heart. This action will slow the loss of blood. If you get cut in the leg, do not stand or walk. This will worsen the injury and increase the loss of blood. Instead, crawl to get help or call for assistance.

If the knife is lodged in your body, first stabilize the weapon. Do not pull it out! Leave the knife where it is and seek medical attention immediately. Many people have walked into hospital emergency rooms with a knife stuck in a major organ and survived because of tamponading - when the surrounding organ tissue surrounds the knife, and blood loss slows down dramatically.

If you think you may have broken a bone or torn a joint during the fight, immobilize the limb immediately. This will reduce the pain significantly and prevent further injury to the afflicted area. These are just a few suggestions that will hopefully buy you some time before the ambulance arrives. It is also a good idea to be prepared for any emergency situation by obtaining emergency first-aid training.

Contact The Police

Your next priority is to contact the police. In most cities, all you need to do is dial 911 to speak with emergency personnel. When you speak to the dispatcher, remain calm and rational, take a deep breath, collect your thoughts, and briefly tell him or her what happened. Give the exact address or location of where the incident took place. If you must leave the crime scene to contact the police, try to remember the exact street address.

If your assailant escaped from the scene, write down his description. Be sure to include his height, weight, clothing, weapon, car model, license tag number, or anything else that might assist the police in apprehending him. Jotting down this information is important because the shock of a violent altercation usually makes victims forget many important details about the attacker and the crime itself.

When the officers arrive at the scene, identify yourself as the victim. *Do not greet the officer with your knife in your hand!* The officers will almost always ask some preliminary questions, such as your name and age and where you live and work. They will then ask you exactly what happened. Explain the sequence of events that led to the knife fight. If the assailant said anything to you, be certain to tell the officers. You will also need to give a complete and accurate description of your assailant. Don't be offended if the officers ask intrusive, seemingly offensive questions. They are just doing their job. Another important point to keep in mind: do not get angry or hostile if the police take 20 minutes to respond to your phone call. They are very busy and usually understaffed.

Save physical evidence

If you want your knife fighting foe to be apprehended and convicted, don't clean up after an attack. You don't want to destroy any physical evidence of the crime. If you were attacked in your home or workplace, do not move, clean, or discard anything until the police have arrived and made a full report of the incident. Broken windows, forced locks, overturned furniture, blood, hair, dirt, mud, etc., are important evidence. To preserve the assailant's fingerprints, avoid touching anything that he might have touched.

Get a good lawyer

Don't forget the legal ramifications of a knife fight. Many people think that street criminals can only destroy them by traditional methods such as murder, rape, assault, and robbery. What they don't know is that the criminal attacker can also sue you. That's right! Anybody can sue anybody for anything. Even the street criminal can find a legal basis for suit, as incredible as that might seem.

The unfortunate fact is that sometimes justice is not served. There are numerous horror stories of decent people who successfully defended themselves against violent attack, only to end up being sued! As a result, the victims had to compensate their attackers financially for injuring them. Ironically, some citizens have also spent time in jail, even though they were only acting in self-defense. Martial arts experts should be particularly careful when defending themselves against criminals. If you are not careful, you can be financially ruined by a criminal, even if you prove your innocence. The legal fees alone can run into thousands of dollars.

You need to be prepared for a possible legal fight. If you are forced into a knife fight and have defended yourself successfully or if you have injured your attacker in the process of defending yourself, it is essential that you plan some type of legal strategy in case the criminal does decide to sue you for damages.

Now is the time for you to find a good attorney who can represent you if the situation arises. You should select an attorney with the same care as you would choose a surgeon for a difficult operation. Make certain that your attorney specializes in criminal law. Find out his or her credentials and record. Most importantly, you want a lawyer who can be reached when you need him or her the most.

Post-traumatic syndrome

Whether you are the victor or the victim, a knife fighting encounter with a criminal attacker will almost always change you in some basic ways. Depending on who you are, the emotional trauma of a knife fight can either strengthen or destroy you.

If you are forced into a knife fight, you may experience a variety of debilitating symptoms. Depending on the severity of the encounter, you may suffer from denial, shock, fear, anger, or severe depression. You may also experience eating and sleeping disorders, societal withdrawal and paranoia. The emotional residuals of a knife fight can also be taxing on your family. Marriages and personal relationships are often destroyed.

Even if you've justifiably crippled or killed your attacker, you may still experience emotional residuals. Contrary to popular belief, justifiably killing another human being, even in the act of self-defense, isn't easy to live with. In the days and weeks after your confrontation, you may experience insomnia, nightmares, depression, guilt, lack of concentration, and anxiety. Consider the many police officers who experience post-trauma from an explosive shoot-out with an armed criminal. Even the veteran officer is not immune to the horrors of violence.

It is, therefore, essential to discuss your experience and feelings with someone you can trust. Someone who will listen with care and empathize with your situation. In most cases, you will need to speak with a professional counselor who is specifically trained to deal with your experience. Psychologists can also help you deal with the emotional trauma of violence. Please don't feel apprehensive to speak with them. They are professionals and will be confidential. Refrain from seeking counseling from your spouse, friends, or family members. They mean well but are unprepared to handle the emotional rigors of your situation.

Revenge

Whenever you successfully defend yourself during a knife fight, there is always the possibility that your assailant will one day come back and seek revenge. The same applies to victims who testify against their attackers in court. There are many incarcerated criminals who patiently wait for the day they are released so they can seek revenge. Other criminals might not harm you directly. Instead, they might terrorize your family, kidnap your child, destroy your property, or mutilate your cat or dog. Depending on the criminal, there's no telling how twisted his actions will be.

If you cripple or kill your attacker or cause him to be imprisoned, there is also the possibility that his friends or immediate family will retaliate. This is particularly dangerous because you have no idea who they are, what they look like, or how many of them exist. The best advice to avoid any type of revenge or retaliation is to avoid disclosing any information about yourself or your family. If your showdown with a criminal was newsworthy, stay clear of the media. You don't want your name mentioned on the six o'clock news or written in the daily newspaper.

The bottom line is: once you fight back (physically or legally) against any criminal, there will always be the menacing possibility that someone will come for you.

Knife Fighting Targets

Chapter 5
Knife Targeting Training

Knife Fighting Targets

Practice Makes Survivors

All the information in the world is useless unless you put it into action. Knife fighting targeting practice is critical! Remember, practice makes perfect, and perfect makes survivors.

Therefore, you'll need to perform your knife targeting techniques, maneuvers and tactic repeatedly in order to master them and make them instinctual. You'll need to set aside some time from your busy schedule to practice and refine your edged weapon skills.

Safe and Effective Knife Training

When it comes to knife fighting training, safety is of paramount importance. Unfortunately, some practitioners will avoid using safety equipment because of big egos, laziness, ignorance and a variety of other reasons. However, I strongly encourage you to take the proper safety precautions.

Here are a few suggestions to help minimize the possibilities of injury when knife training:

1. Never, ever practice with real knives.

2. Buy the best knife training equipment that you can afford.

3. Have a trained expert show you the proper way to use the equipment.

4. Regularly inspect your training knife and eye protection for wear and defects.

Knife Fighting Targets

5. Be especially alert when training with someone with less skill or experience.

6. Be very cautious when performing knife training drills for the first time.

The only effective method of developing knife fighting targeting skills is to practice safely with a training partner. There are numerous training knives on the market. When looking to purchase training knives, avoid buying those rubber knives that wiggle when you move them. These knives are cheap and very unrealistic.

Also, be exceptionally careful when slashing at your partner's face. To prevent eye injuries, wear some eye protection. Again, *never practice with real knives.*

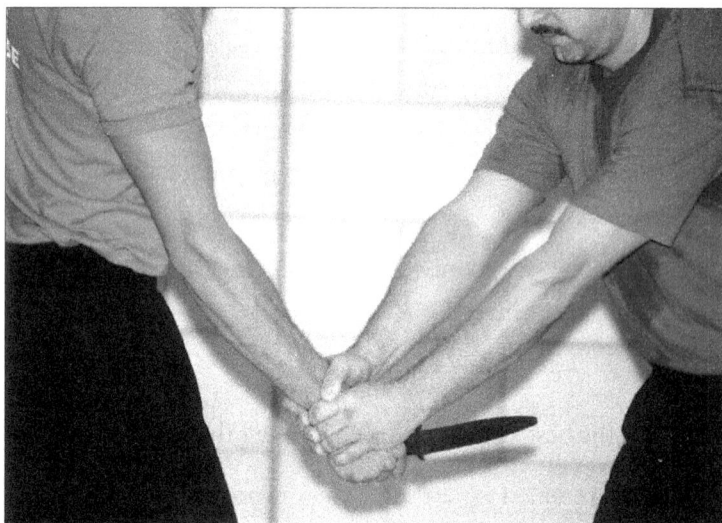

If you are going to workout with a rubber training knife, be certain to use one that is made of hard rubber.

Realism is the key to your Survival

Knife targeting workouts must be completely realistic. Anything less could spell disaster for you when a real situation occurs. You must methodically integrate the frightening and spontaneous elements of combat safely into your workout routine. Such reality-based training is a sure fire method of preparing you for the real thing.

For example, frequently conduct simulated knife fights with your training partner in cramped and unfamiliar environments. Train in the rain, in the snow, in the mud, etc.

Since no two knife fights are ever the same, you need to incorporate a wide variety of combative scenarios into your training program. This realistic and dynamic form of training will provide you with the experience necessary to handle the unpredictable nature of knife combat. Remember, inadequate or unrealistic training is a waste of time and extremely dangerous for you. Always train for the reality of combat.

Finally, when purchasing knife training gear, spare no expense. Edged weapon training is a serious matter, and your training gear should reflect it. Good equipment will provide years of reliable use and significantly enhance your skills.

Knife fighting gear

Edged weapon training is a serious matter, and your training gear should reflect it. Good equipment will provide years of reliable use and significantly enhance your edged weapon skills. Here is a brief list of the training gear that you will need: training knife, protective wrist cuff, safety glasses, mouth guard. Let's take a quick look at each one.

The Training Knife

A training knife or "trainer" is a professionally crafted training knife that is similar to a real combat knife, except the blade has no edge and the tip has been rounded for safety purposes.

Training knives are very realistic, so always consult with the local laws in your area concerning the practice of knife training and carrying of simulated edged weapons.

When performing various knife fighting drills and targeting exercises with your training knife, be cognizant of the *grouping of your cuts.* Grouping means your cuts are clustered closely together during a particular drill or exercise. There are two types of grouping classifications: Proximity and Depth.

Some training knives feature a chalk mark delivery system that will allow you to see the grouping of cuts.

If you are planning on working on fixed blade training, there are several excellent rubber knives on the market. These training knives allow you to chalk the edges so you can see the grouping of your cuts.

If you are planning on practicing with tactical folders, Spyderco has produced some quality training knives.

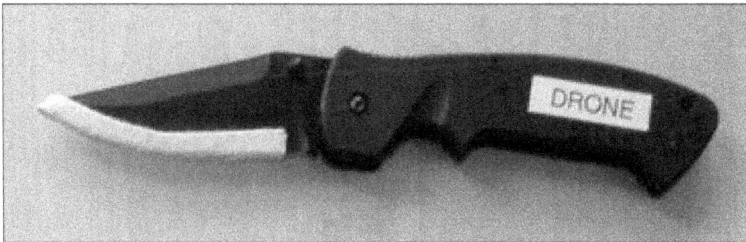

Pictured here, a custom made training knife with a chalk mark delivery system.

Protective Wrist Cuff

Being repeatedly struck on your wrists with a training knife is no picnic. As a matter of fact, it can actually damage your wrists. Therefore, it's in your best interest to have some type of wrist protection. The best solution is a thick three-inch plastic or leather wrist cuff that will stay securely on your wrist during various knife fighting exercises. Unfortunately, these protective wrist cuffs are not available on the market, so you'll have to make them yourself.

Pictured here, a custom-made protective wrist cuff.

Safety Glasses

Let me make this perfectly clear from the start, eye protection is critical when participating in any form of knife fighting training. Do not take the risk of losing your eyesight! Always where eye protection at all times! Also, be certain your safety glasses are shatter proof and will sufficiently cover both of your eyes.

Mouth guard

Finally, you are going to need a mouth guard that is made of durable rubber that will protect your teeth when knife sparring. There are two types that can be used when knife training: single and double. The mouthpiece is a vital and often overlooked piece of safety equipment that can help prevent the following injuries:

1. The mouthpiece helps prevent a broken jaw by bracing it together if you are accidentally hit on the chin.

2. Getting your teeth chipped or knocked out.

3. Biting your tongue or lips.

Knife fighting drills and exercises

There are literally dozens of different knife fighting drills. Here are just a few exercises that can help you get a jump start on your training.

Mirror knife training

In front of a mirror, practice linear and lateral footwork movements with a training knife in your hand. This should be performed from both your right and left stances. Be aware of your stance as you move, keep your weight evenly distributed, keep your balance, and stay relaxed. This should be practiced on all different types of terrain (wet grass, mud, ice, wet pavement, snow, gravel, and sand).

You must also practice the knife fighting stance until it becomes instinctual. This means that you will have to practice in front of a full-length mirror. When you assume your stance, scrutinize yourself and pick out the strategic deficiencies. For example, what targets are exposed? Is your balance sacrificed? Are your knees bent? Is your knife close to your body at all times?

Knife Fighting Flow Drills

Knife fighting targeting skills can be improved by adding flow drills to your training. They are excellent for developing timing, speed, and target accuracy. If you're just starting out, I strongly suggest practicing the drills with a kubotan first, then later on you can switch over to a training knife. Again, never use real knives.

Hubod Drill (ice pick vertical stab)

Step 1: The two practitioners begin the hubod drill with the man on the left initiating a tight overhead stab. The man on the right blocks his arm.

Step 2: After blocking the attack, the man on the right uses his right arm to redirect his partner's arm.

Step 3: The man on the right redirects his partners arm and slaps it downward with his left hand.

Step 4: The man on the right attacks his partner with a tight overhead stab.

Step 5: Next, the man on the left blocks his partner's attack and redirects it with his right arm.

Step 6: He redirects his partners arm and slaps it downward with his left hand.

Step 7: The cycle is complete, the man on the left begins again with a tight overhead stab.

Horizontal Stabbing Drill

Step 1: The two men square off with each other.

Step 2: Next, the man on the left delivers a controlled eye stab towards his partner's face. His partner intercepts the attack with the palm of his hand.

Step 3: The man on the right redirects his partner's arm downward.

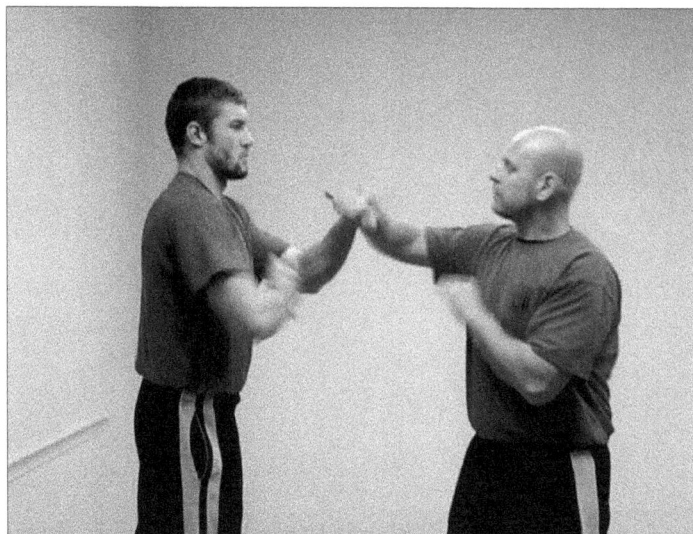

Step 4: And counters with a stab to his partner's face.

Step 5: The man on the left intercepts his partner's attack and redirects it downward.

Step 6: The cycle is complete with the man on the left delivering another attack.

Combining Flow Drills

You can also combine these flow drills together. Keep in mind, this is done arbitrarily with no set pattern. Remember, your goal is to flow with your weapon, so keep it alive and dynamic!

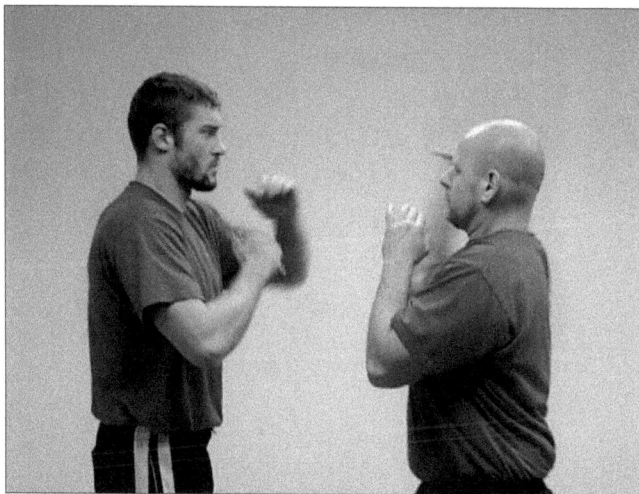

Step 1: The man on the right begins with hubod.

Step 2: The man (right) initiates a tight ice pick stab. The man on the left blocks it.

Step 3: Next, the man on the left redirects his partner's arm.

Step 4: He slaps his partner's arm downward.

Step 5: He counters with a tight overhead stab. The man on the right blocks the attack.

Step 6: The man on the right redirects his partner's arm.

Step 7: And slaps it.

Step 8: The man on the right transitions to the back hand stabbing drill.

Step 9: The man on the left intercepts his partner's attack and redirects it downward.

Step 10: He counters with a stab.

Step 11: The man on the right intercepts the attack.

Step 12: He counters with an overhead stab, transitioning back to the hubod drill.

Knife Sparring

Knife sparring is a one of the most effective methods for developing knife targeting skills. It also develops many physical attributes like speed, quickness, coordination, agility, timing, distancing, ambidexterity, endurance, tactile sensitivity, finesse, accuracy, and non-telegraphic movement.

Knife sparring skills require combining various slashing and stabbing combinations into logical combinations. Basic knife sparring sessions are conducted at a moderate and controlled pace. You can perform these sparring sessions just about anywhere, such as a gym, basement, garage and even outdoors. However, before you begin training, you'll need some equipment. At the bare minimum, you'll need eye protection, safety training knives, protective wrist cuff, and a mouth piece.

Depending on your level of conditioning, sparring rounds can range anywhere from one to five minutes. Each round is separated by either 30-second, one-minute or two-minute breaks. A good sparring session consists of at least five to eight rounds.

Since knife sparring workouts are structured around time, you will need a good workout timer. Most workout timers will allow you to adjust your round lengths anywhere from 30 seconds to 9 minutes. Rest periods can be changed from 30 seconds to 5 minutes depending on your level of conditioning and training goals.

While knife sparring is vital component of edged weapon training, it is important to integrate this form of training at the proper time. Never participate in knife sparring until you have acquired some of the following skills.

1. You must possess a variety of offensive and defensive knife fighting techniques that can be applied quickly and effectively.

2. You must demonstrate the ability to control the force of both slashing and stabbing techniques.

3. You must possess the fundamental attributes of knife combat, including speed, timing, coordination, accuracy, balance, and non-telegraphic movement.

4. Both you and your training partner must possess a safe and mature attitude toward knife training. Remember, prematurely engaging in knife sparring can be dangerous.

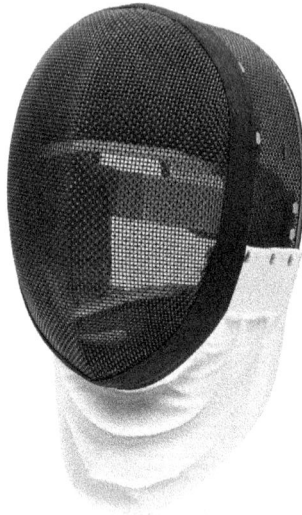

As an additional safety measure, you can use a fencing mask when knife sparring with your partner.

Non-dominant hand knife training

When practicing knife targeting skills, always devote sufficient time to your non-dominant hand. Ambidexterity is an invaluable skill and here are just a few reasons why your weak hand should be developed:

1. There is always the possibility that your strong hand might be injured in a knife fight and you will be forced to use your weak hand.

2. It enhances your overall confidence.

3. It reinforces good knife fighting skills.

4. It can be useful if your dominant hand becomes occupied during the knife fight.

Practice in close quarters

You should also spend adequate time learning how to use your knife in close-quarter environments. Here are just a few examples:

1. In your car.

2. In an elevator.

3. On a bridge.

4. In a narrow hallway.

5. In a doorway.

6. In a bathroom stall.

7. In a crowd.

8. In a cluttered garage.

9. On a narrow stairwell.

10. Between tall shrubbery

Knife Retention training

There's a good possibility that a knife fight will end up in a struggle with the adversary. In fact, the vast majority of knife fighting simulations conducted in my school usually end up the two students struggling to control each other's weapon.

This brings up the important issue of knife retention skills. You must know how to effectively counter various types of traps, grabs and disarm techniques. Never pick up a knife unless you are absolutely confident that you can maintain complete control over it at all times. Remember, if you drop your knife, you might very well lose your life.

Two of the best ways of improving your weapon retention skills is performing grip strengthening exercises and also practice the knife struggle drill.

The knife struggle drill

I created the knife struggle drill for two important reasons:

1. To improve your own weapon retention skills.

2. To efficiently escape and counter wrist grabs when your adversary attempts to control your knife.

You can perform the knife struggle drill by following these steps:

1. Remember to always use a training knife and eye protection when performing this drill.

2. Begin with both you and your training partner in close-quarter knife fighting range and with your training knives held in the hammer grip.

3. Assume 45-degeree angled stances with your body weight evenly distributed over each leg.

4. Next, firmly grab hold of each others wrist (the one that is holding the training knife).

5. Grip each others wrist with a moderate amount of pressure that prevents your knives from stabbing each other. You can test the grip pressure by pushing and pulling back and fourth with your knife.

6. Throughout the entire drill, both you and your partner will need to constantly maintain forward pressure with your knives.

7. Next, you and your training partner and going to take turns escaping from the wrist grab. If you are holding your knife in your right hand, your escape is accomplished by rotating your knife and wrist in a tight and fluid counter-clockwise motion. This action breaks your partners hold and frees your knife.

Knife Fighting Targets

8. Eventually, you can progressively increase the pressure of the wrist grab to make this drill even more challenging.

9. Perform this drill for a duration of 5-10 minutes.

Petroleum jelly

If you want to replicate the sweat, blood and grim that often accompanies a knife fight, rub a liberal amount of petroleum jelly on your hands prior to training. Not only will this test the integrity of your grip, it will also teach you how to improvise your knife fighting skills when faced with adverse conditions.

Just remember, this type of knife fighting training is very challenging and should only be used by experienced practitioners who possess a strong foundation in edged weapon combat.

Disability Training

Disability training is designed to help you experience what it's like to knife fight when you are under the weather or temporarily handicapped. Here are a few suggestions that will help get you started.

1. Practice when you're plagued with a migraine headache.

2. Practice knife fighting when confined to a wheelchair.

3. Knife spar with one arm in a sling.

4. Practice knife skills while standing on crutches.

5. Engage in ground knife fighting when you are feeling fatigued or exhausted.

6. Practice knife weapon retention while you are blindfolded.

7. Knife spar while wearing a weight vest.

8. Wear an elevation training mask when knife sparring.

9. Want to experience some real physical discomfort, practice

knife training drills with a marble in your shoe.

10. Knife fight with you non-dominant hand against your partners dominant hand.

Defend From Different Positions

There are nine general positions in which you can knife fight. Make it a habit to practice with your partner until the two of you are comfortable and proficient with all of the positions. They include the following:

1. Both you and your partner are prone.

2. You are kneeling and your partner is prone.

3. Your partner is kneeling and you are prone.

4. Both you and your partner are kneeling.

5. You are standing and your partner is prone.

6. Your partner is standing and you are prone.

7. You are standing and your partner is kneeling.

8. Your partner is standing and you are kneeling.

9. Both you and your partner are standing.

Videotaping your workouts

If you really want to actually see your progress, videotape your knife fighting workouts. The video footage will provide you with a more accurate picture of what you are doing in your training. You will be able to observe mistakes and recognize your strengths and weaknesses. The video will also motivate you to train harder. Remember to date each video clip; later on you will be able to compare and see marked improvements in your training performance.

Reading and Research

The intellectual, or academic, aspects of knife fighting training cannot be overstated. You must possess an insatiable desire to learn and grow to your full potential. Academic research involves voracious reading. The body of printed materials on knife fighting has grown astronomically.

Try to read anything you can get your hands on, provided the author is reputable and experienced in the field of knife combat. A word of caution! Be especially leery of indie authors who have little or no background in the field of combat sciences. In most cases, these charlatans are simply parroting information from other sources and claiming it as their own. Remember, when it comes to knife fighting (or any form of self-defense) the author's qualifications, reputation, and experience matters!

Also, don't make the common mistake of passively reading material. Get into the habit of dissecting and noting literature. Strategically sound knife fighting theories and unique training concepts should be noted and remembered. Books should be read over and over again until practical ideas are intellectually solidified. Finally, always read material with an open mind balanced with healthy skepticism.

Knife Fighting Conditioning

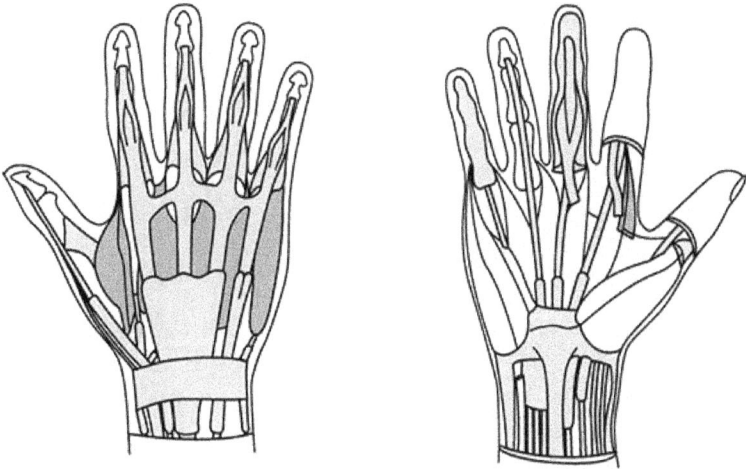

Grip Strength

Grip strength is a vital component of knife fighting. In fact, strong fingers, wrists and forearms can make all the difference between life and death in a knife fight.

Powerful hands and forearms will also amplify the speed and power of your slashing and stabbing techniques. Most importantly, strong forearms will dramatically enhance your knife retention skills and enhance your ability to control the assailant's knife hand. There are several effective hand and forearm exercises you can perform at your leisure to strengthen these important muscles.

What follows are several efficient ways to condition and strengthen your hands, wrists and forearms for the rigors of knife fighting.

Knife Fighting Targets

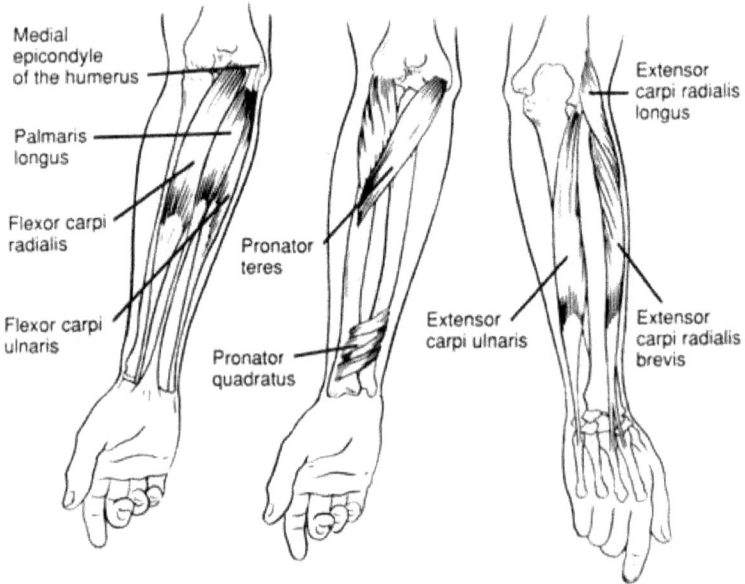

Anatomy of the human forearm.

Tennis Ball

If you are low on cash and just starting out with your training, you can begin by squeezing a tennis ball a couple times per week. One hundred repetitions per hand would be a great start.

You can also perform a "time hold" workout where you would hold your squeeze for approximately five to ten seconds, and then slowly release the pressure. You would repeat this process anywhere from 10 to 15 repetitions. Next, switch the ball to your other hand and start over.

Power Putty

One excellent hand exerciser that strengthens all the muscles in your fingers and hands is Power Putty. Essentially, Power Putty is a flexible silicone rubber that can be squeezed, stretched, and crushed. Begin using the putty for ten minute sessions and progressively build up to thirty minutes.

This tough resistant putty will strengthen the muscles of your forearm, wrists, hands and fingers. Remember to work both hands equally.

Hand Grippers

Another effective way to strengthen your hands, wrists and forearms is to work out with heavy duty hand grippers. While there are a wide selection of them on the market, I personally prefer using the Captains of Crush brand. These high quality grippers are virtually indestructible and they are sold in a variety of different resistance levels ranging from 60 to 365 pounds.

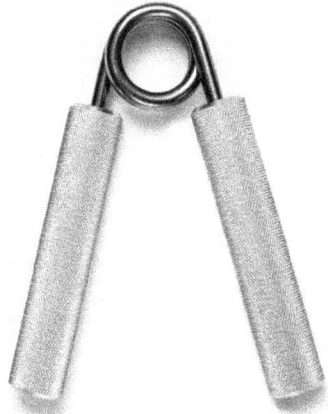

Weight Training

Finally, you can also condition your wrists and forearms by performing various forearm exercises with free weights. Exercises like: hammer curls, reverse curls, wrist curls, and reverse wrist curls are great for developing powerful forearms. When training your forearms, be certain to work both your extensor and flexor muscles. Let's look at some of the exercises.

Barbell Wrist Curls

This exercise strengthens the flexor muscles. Perform 5 sets of 8-10 repetitions. To perform the exercise, follow these steps:

1. Sit at the end of a bench, grab a barbell with an underhand grip and place both of your hands close together.

2. In a smooth and controlled fashion, slowly bend your wrists and lower the barbell toward the floor.

3. Contract your forearms and curl the weight back to the starting position.

Reverse Wrist Curls

This exercise develops and strengthens the extensor muscle of the forearm. Perform 6 sets of 6-8 repetitions. To perform the exercise, follow these steps:

1. Sit at the end of a bench, hold a barbell with an overhand grip (your hands should be approximately 11 inches apart) and place your forearms on top of your thighs.

2. Slowly lower the barbell as far as your wrists will allow.

3. Flex your wrists upward back to the starting position.

Behind-the-Back Wrist Curls

This exercise strengthens both the flexor muscles of the forearms. Perform 5 sets of 6-8 repetitions To perform the exercise, follow these steps:

1. Hold a barbell behind your back at arm's length (your hands should be approximately shoulder-width apart).

2. Uncurl your finger and let the barbell slowly roll down your palms.

3. Close your hands and roll the barbell back into your hands.

Hammer Curls

This exercise strengthens both the Brachialis and Brachioradialis muscles. Perform 5 sets of 8-10 repetitions. To perform the exercise, follow these steps:

1. Stand with both feet approximately shoulder width apart, with both dumbbells at your sides.

2. Keeping your elbows close to your body and your palms facing inward, slowly curl both dumbbells upward towards your shoulders.

3. Slowly return to the starting position.

Reverse Barbell Curls

Reverse curls can be a great alternative to hammer curls. This exercise strengthens both the Brachialis and Brachioradialis muscles. Perform 5 sets of 8-10 repetitions. To perform the exercise, follow these steps:

1. Stand with both feet approximately shoulder width apart. Hold a barbell with your palms facing down (pronated grip).

2. Keeping your upper arms stationary, curl the weights up until the bar is at shoulder level.

3. Slowly return to the starting position.

Glossary

The following terms are defined in the context of Contemporary Fighting Arts and its related concepts. In many instances, the definitions bear little resemblance to those found in a standard dictionary.

A

accuracy—The precise or exact projection of force. Accuracy is also defined as the ability to execute a combative movement with precision and exactness.

adaptability—The ability to physically and psychologically adjust to new or different conditions or circumstances of combat.

advanced first-strike tools—Offensive techniques that are specifically used when confronted with multiple opponents.

aerobic exercise—Literally, "with air." Exercise that elevates the heart rate to a training level for a prolonged period of time, usually 30 minutes.

affective preparedness – One of the three components of preparedness. Affective preparedness means being emotionally, philosophically, and spiritually prepared for the strains of combat. See cognitive preparedness and psychomotor preparedness.

aggression—Hostile and injurious behavior directed toward a person.

aggressive response—One of the three possible counters when assaulted by a grab, choke, or hold from a standing position. Aggressive response requires you to counter the enemy with destructive blows and strikes. See moderate response and passive response.

aggressive hand positioning—Placement of hands so as to imply aggressive or hostile intentions.

agility—An attribute of combat. One's ability to move his or her body quickly and gracefully.

amalgamation—A scientific process of uniting or merging.

ambidextrous—The ability to perform with equal facility on both the right and left sides of the body.

anabolic steroids – synthetic chemical compounds that resemble the male sex hormone testosterone. This performance-enhancing drug is known to increase lean muscle mass, strength, and endurance.

analysis and integration—One of the five elements of CFA's mental component. This is the painstaking process of breaking down various elements, concepts, sciences, and disciplines into their atomic parts, and then methodically and strategically analyzing, experimenting, and drastically modifying the information so that it fulfills three combative requirements: efficiency, effectiveness, and safety. Only then is it finally integrated into the CFA system.

anatomical striking targets—The various anatomical body targets that can be struck and which are especially vulnerable to potential harm. They include: the eyes, temple, nose, chin, back of neck, front of neck, solar plexus, ribs, groin, thighs, knees, shins, and instep.

anchoring – The strategic process of trapping the assailant's neck or limb in order to control the range of engagement during razing.

assailant—A person who threatens or attacks another person.

assault—The threat or willful attempt to inflict injury upon the person of another.

assault and battery—The unlawful touching of another person without justification.

assessment—The process of rapidly gathering, analyzing, and accurately evaluating information in terms of threat and danger. You can assess people, places, actions, and objects.

attack—Offensive action designed to physically control, injure, or kill another person.

attack by combination (ABC) - One of the five methods of attack. See compound attack.

attack by drawing (ABD) - One of the five methods of attack. A method of attack predicated on counterattack.

attitude—One of the three factors that determine who wins a street fight. Attitude means being emotionally, philosophically, and spiritually liberated from societal and religious mores. See skills and knowledge.

attributes of combat—The physical, mental, and spiritual qualities that enhance combat skills and tactics.

awareness—Perception or knowledge of people, places, actions, and objects. (In CFA, there are three categories of tactical awareness: criminal awareness, situational awareness, and self-awareness.)

B

balance—One's ability to maintain equilibrium while stationary or moving.

blading the body—Strategically positioning your body at a 45-degree angle.

blitz and disengage—A style of sparring whereby a fighter moves into a range of combat, unleashes a strategic compound attack, and then quickly disengages to a safe distance. Of all sparring methodologies, the blitz and disengage most closely resembles a real street fight.

block—A defensive tool designed to intercept the assailant's attack by placing a non-vital target between the assailant's strike and your vital body target.

body composition—The ratio of fat to lean body tissue.

body language—Nonverbal communication through posture, gestures, and facial expressions.

body mechanics—Technically precise body movement during the execution of a body weapon, defensive technique, or other fighting maneuver.

body tackle – A tackle that occurs when your opponent haphazardly rushes forward and plows his body into yours.

body weapon—Also known as a tool, one of the various body parts that can be used to strike or otherwise injure or kill a criminal assailant.

burn out—A negative emotional state acquired by physically over- training. Some symptoms include: illness, boredom, anxiety, disinterest in training, and general sluggishness.

C

cadence—Coordinating tempo and rhythm to establish a timing pattern of movement.

cardiorespiratory conditioning—The component of physical fitness that deals with the heart, lungs, and circulatory system.

centerline—An imaginary vertical line that divides your body in half and which contains many of your vital anatomical targets.

choke holds—Holds that impair the flow of blood or oxygen to the brain.

circular movements—Movements that follow the direction of a curve.

close-quarter combat—One of the three ranges of knife and

bludgeon combat. At this distance, you can strike, slash, or stab your assailant with a variety of close-quarter techniques.

cognitive development—One of the five elements of CFA's mental component. The process of developing and enhancing your fighting skills through specific mental exercises and techniques. See analysis and integration, killer instinct, philosophy, and strategic/tactical development.

cognitive exercises—Various mental exercises used to enhance fighting skills and tactics.

cognitive preparedness – One of the three components of preparedness. Cognitive preparedness means being equipped with the strategic concepts, principles, and general knowledge of combat. See affective preparedness and psychomotor preparedness.

combat-oriented training—Training that is specifically related to the harsh realities of both armed and unarmed combat. See ritual-oriented training and sport-oriented training.

combative arts—The various arts of war. See martial arts.

combative attributes—See attributes of combat.

combative fitness—A state characterized by cardiorespiratory and muscular/skeletal conditioning, as well as proper body composition.

combative mentality—Also known as the killer instinct, this is a combative state of mind necessary for fighting. See killer instinct.

combat ranges—The various ranges of unarmed combat.

combative utility—The quality of condition of being combatively useful.

combination(s)—See compound attack.

common peroneal nerve—A pressure point area located approximately four to six inches above the knee on the midline of the outside of the thigh.

composure—A combative attribute. Composure is a quiet and focused mind-set that enables you to acquire your combative agenda.

compound attack—One of the five conventional methods of attack. Two or more body weapons launched in strategic succession whereby the fighter overwhelms his assailant with a flurry of full speed, full-force blows.

conditioning training—A CFA training methodology requiring the practitioner to deliver a variety of offensive and defensive combinations for a 4-minute period. See proficiency training and street training.

contact evasion—Physically moving or manipulating your body to avoid being tackled by the adversary.

Contemporary Fighting Arts—A modern martial art and self-defense system made up of three parts: physical, mental, and spiritual.

conventional ground-fighting tools—Specific ground-fighting techniques designed to control, restrain, and temporarily incapacitate your adversary. Some conventional ground fighting tactics include: submission holds, locks, certain choking techniques, and specific striking techniques.

coordination—A physical attribute characterized by the ability to perform a technique or movement with efficiency, balance, and accuracy.

counterattack—Offensive action made to counter an assailant's initial attack.

courage—A combative attribute. The state of mind and spirit that enables a fighter to face danger and vicissitudes with confidence, resolution, and bravery.

creatine monohydrate—A tasteless and odorless white powder that mimics some of the effects of anabolic steroids. Creatine is a safe body-building product that can benefit anyone who wants to increase their strength, endurance, and lean muscle mass.

criminal awareness—One of the three categories of CFA awareness. It involves a general understanding and knowledge of the nature and dynamics of a criminal's motivations, mentalities, methods, and capabilities to perpetrate violent crime. See situational awareness and self-awareness.

criminal justice—The study of criminal law and the procedures associated with its enforcement.

criminology—The scientific study of crime and criminals.

cross-stepping—The process of crossing one foot in front of or behind the other when moving.

crushing tactics—Nuclear grappling-range techniques designed to crush the assailant's anatomical targets.

D

deadly force—Weapons or techniques that may result in unconsciousness, permanent disfigurement, or death.

deception—A combative attribute. A stratagem whereby you delude your assailant.

decisiveness—A combative attribute. The ability to follow a tactical course of action that is unwavering and focused.

defense—The ability to strategically thwart an assailant's attack (armed or unarmed).

defensive flow—A progression of continuous defensive responses.

defensive mentality—A defensive mind-set.

defensive reaction time—The elapsed time between an assailant's physical attack and your defensive response to that attack. See offensive reaction time.

demeanor—A person's outward behavior. One of the essential factors to consider when assessing a threatening individual.

diet—A lifestyle of healthy eating.

disingenuous vocalization—The strategic and deceptive utilization of words to successfully launch a preemptive strike at your adversary.

distancing—The ability to quickly understand spatial relationships and how they relate to combat.

distractionary tactics—Various verbal and physical tactics designed to distract your adversary.

double-end bag—A small leather ball hung from the ceiling and anchored to the floor with bungee cord. It helps develop striking accuracy, speed, timing, eye-hand coordination, footwork and overall defensive skills.

double-leg takedown—A takedown that occurs when your opponent shoots for both of your legs to force you to the ground.

E

ectomorph—One of the three somatotypes. A body type characterized by a high degree of slenderness, angularity, and fragility. See endomorph and mesomorph.

effectiveness—One of the three criteria for a CFA body weapon, technique, tactic, or maneuver. It means the ability to produce a desired effect. See efficiency and safety.

efficiency—One of the three criteria for a CFA body weapon, technique, tactic, or maneuver. It means the ability to reach an objective quickly and economically. See effectiveness and safety.

emotionless—A combative attribute. Being temporarily devoid of human feeling.

endomorph—One of the three somatotypes. A body type characterized by a high degree of roundness, softness, and body fat. See ectomorph and mesomorph.

evasion—A defensive maneuver that allows you to strategically maneuver your body away from the assailant's strike.

evasive sidestepping—Evasive footwork where the practitioner moves to either the right or left side.

evasiveness—A combative attribute. The ability to avoid threat or danger.

excessive force—An amount of force that exceeds the need for a particular event and is unjustified in the eyes of the law.

experimentation—The painstaking process of testing a combative hypothesis or theory.

explosiveness—A combative attribute that is characterized by a sudden outburst of violent energy.

F

fear—A strong and unpleasant emotion caused by the anticipation or awareness of threat or danger. There are three stages of fear in order of intensity: fright, panic, and terror. See fright, panic, and terror.

feeder—A skilled technician who manipulates the focus mitts.

femoral nerve—A pressure point area located approximately 6 inches above the knee on the inside of the thigh.

fighting stance—Any one of the stances used in CFA's system. A strategic posture you can assume when face-to-face with an unarmed assailant(s). The fighting stance is generally used after you have launched your first-strike tool.

fight-or-flight syndrome—A response of the sympathetic nervous system to a fearful and threatening situation, during which it prepares your body to either fight or flee from the perceived danger.

finesse—A combative attribute. The ability to skillfully execute a movement or a series of movements with grace and refinement.

first strike—Proactive force used to interrupt the initial stages of an assault before it becomes a self-defense situation.

first-strike principle—A CFA principle that states that when physical danger is imminent and you have no other tactical option but to fight back, you should strike first, strike fast, and strike with authority and keep the pressure on.

first-strike stance—One of the stances used in CFA's system. A strategic posture used prior to initiating a first strike.

first-strike tools—Specific offensive tools designed to initiate a preemptive strike against your adversary.

fisted blows – Hand blows delivered with a clenched fist.

five tactical options – The five strategic responses you can make in a self-defense situation, listed in order of increasing level of resistance: comply, escape, de-escalate, assert, and fight back.

flexibility—The muscles' ability to move through maximum natural ranges. See muscular/skeletal conditioning.

focus mitts—Durable leather hand mitts used to develop and sharpen offensive and defensive skills.

footwork—Quick, economical steps performed on the balls of the feet while you are relaxed, alert, and balanced. Footwork is structured around four general movements: forward, backward, right, and left.

fractal tool—Offensive or defensive tools that can be used in more than one combat range.

fright—The first stage of fear; quick and sudden fear. See panic and terror.

full Beat – One of the four beat classifications in the Widow Maker Program. The full beat strike has a complete initiation and retraction phase.

G

going postal - a slang term referring to a person who suddenly and unexpectedly attacks you with an explosive and frenzied flurry of blows. Also known as postal attack.

grappling range—One of the three ranges of unarmed combat. Grappling range is the closest distance of unarmed combat from which you can employ a wide variety of close-quarter tools and techniques. The grappling range of unarmed combat is also divided into two planes: vertical (standing) and horizontal (ground fighting). See kicking range and punching range.

grappling-range tools—The various body tools and techniques that are employed in the grappling range of unarmed combat, including head butts; biting, tearing, clawing, crushing, and gouging tactics; foot stomps, horizontal, vertical, and diagonal elbow strikes, vertical and diagonal knee strikes, chokes, strangles, joint locks, and holds. See punching range tools and kicking range tools.

ground fighting—Also known as the horizontal grappling plane, this is fighting that takes place on the ground.

guard—Also known as the hand guard, this refers to a fighter's hand positioning.

guard position—Also known as leg guard or scissors hold, this is a ground-fighting position in which a fighter is on his back holding his opponent between his legs.

H

half beat – One of the four beat classifications in the Widow Maker Program. The half beat strike is delivered through the retraction phase of the proceeding strike.

hand immobilization attack (HIA) - One of the five methods of attack. A method of attack whereby the practitioner traps his opponent's limb or limbs in order to execute an offense attack of his own.

hand positioning—See guard.

hand wraps—Long strips of cotton that are wrapped around the hands and wrists for greater protection.

haymaker—A wild and telegraphed swing of the arms executed by an unskilled fighter.

head-hunter—A fighter who primarily attacks the head.

heavy bag—A large cylindrical bag used to develop kicking, punching, or striking power.

high-line kick—One of the two different classifications of a kick. A kick that is directed to targets above an assailant's waist level. See low-line kick.

hip fusing—A full-contact drill that teaches a fighter to "stand his ground" and overcome the fear of exchanging blows with a stronger opponent. This exercise is performed by connecting two fighters with a 3-foot chain, forcing them to fight in the punching range of unarmed combat.

histrionics—The field of theatrics or acting.

hook kick—A circular kick that can be delivered in both kicking and punching ranges.

hook punch—A circular punch that can be delivered in both the punching and grappling ranges.

I

impact power—Destructive force generated by mass and velocity.

impact training—A training exercise that develops pain tolerance.

incapacitate—To disable an assailant by rendering him unconscious or damaging his bones, joints, or organs.

initiative—Making the first offensive move in combat.

inside position—The area between the opponent's arms, where he has the greatest amount of control.

intent—One of the essential factors to consider when assessing a threatening individual. The assailant's purpose or motive. See demeanor, positioning, range, and weapon capability.

intuition—The innate ability to know or sense something without the use of rational thought.

J

jeet kune do (JKD) - "Way of the intercepting fist." Bruce Lee's approach to the martial arts, which includes his innovative concepts, theories, methodologies, and philosophies.

jersey Pull – Strategically pulling the assailant's shirt or jacket over his head as he disengages from the clinch position.

joint lock—A grappling-range technique that immobilizes the assailant's joint.

K

kick—A sudden, forceful strike with the foot.

kicking range—One of the three ranges of unarmed combat. Kicking range is the furthest distance of unarmed combat wherein you use your legs to strike an assailant. See grappling range and punching range.

kicking-range tools—The various body weapons employed in the kicking range of unarmed combat, including side kicks, push kicks, hook kicks, and vertical kicks.

killer instinct—A cold, primal mentality that surges to your consciousness and turns you into a vicious fighter.

kinesics—The study of nonlinguistic body movement communications. (For example, eye movement, shrugs, or facial gestures.)

kinesiology—The study of principles and mechanics of human movement.

kinesthetic perception—The ability to accurately feel your body during the execution of a particular movement.

knowledge—One of the three factors that determine who will win a street fight. Knowledge means knowing and understanding how to fight. See skills and attitude.

L

lead side -The side of the body that faces an assailant.

leg guard—See guard position.

linear movement—Movements that follow the path of a straight line.

low-maintenance tool—Offensive and defensive tools that require the least amount of training and practice to maintain proficiency. Low maintenance tools generally do not require preliminary stretching.

low-line kick—One of the two different classifications of a kick. A kick that is directed to targets below the assailant's waist level. (See high-line kick.)

lock—See joint lock.

M

maneuver—To manipulate into a strategically desired position.

MAP—An acronym that stands for moderate, aggressive, passive. MAP provides the practitioner with three possible responses to various grabs, chokes, and holds that occur from a standing position. See aggressive response, moderate response, and passive response.

martial arts—The "arts of war."

masking—The process of concealing your true feelings from your opponent by manipulating and managing your body language.

mechanics—(See body mechanics.)

mental attributes—The various cognitive qualities that enhance your fighting skills.

mental component—One of the three vital components of the CFA system. The mental component includes the cerebral aspects of fighting including the killer instinct, strategic and tactical development, analysis and integration, philosophy, and cognitive development. See physical component and spiritual component.

mesomorph—One of the three somatotypes. A body type classified by a high degree of muscularity and strength. The mesomorph possesses the ideal physique for unarmed combat. See ectomorph and endomorph.

mobility—A combative attribute. The ability to move your body quickly and freely while balanced. See footwork.

moderate response—One of the three possible counters when assaulted by a grab, choke, or hold from a standing position. Moderate response requires you to counter your opponent with a control and restraint (submission hold). See aggressive response and passive response.

modern martial art—A pragmatic combat art that has evolved to meet the demands and characteristics of the present time.

mounted position—A dominant ground-fighting position where a fighter straddles his opponent.

muscular endurance—The muscles' ability to perform the same motion or task repeatedly for a prolonged period of time.

muscular flexibility—The muscles' ability to move through maximum natural ranges.

muscular strength—The maximum force that can be exerted by a particular muscle or muscle group against resistance.

muscular/skeletal conditioning—An element of physical fitness that entails muscular strength, endurance, and flexibility.

N

naked choke—A throat choke executed from the chest to back position. This secure choke is executed with two hands and it can be performed while standing, kneeling, and ground fighting with the opponent.

neck crush – A powerful pain compliance technique used when the adversary buries his head in your chest to avoid being razed.

neutralize—See incapacitate.

neutral zone—The distance outside the kicking range at which neither the practitioner nor the assailant can touch the other.

nonaggressive physiology—Strategic body language used prior to initiating a first strike.

nontelegraphic movement—Body mechanics or movements that do not inform an assailant of your intentions.

nuclear ground-fighting tools—Specific grappling range tools designed to inflict immediate and irreversible damage. Nuclear tools and tactics include biting tactics, tearing tactics, crushing tactics, continuous choking tactics, gouging techniques, raking tactics, and all striking techniques.

O

offense—The armed and unarmed means and methods of attacking a criminal assailant.

offensive flow—Continuous offensive movements (kicks, blows, and strikes) with unbroken continuity that ultimately neutralize or terminate the opponent. See compound attack.

offensive reaction time—The elapsed time between target selection and target impaction.

one-mindedness—A state of deep concentration wherein you are free from all distractions (internal and external).

ostrich defense—One of the biggest mistakes one can make when defending against an opponent. This is when the practitioner looks away from that which he fears (punches, kicks, and strikes). His mentality is, "If I can't see it, it can't hurt me."

P

pain tolerance—Your ability to physically and psychologically withstand pain.

panic—The second stage of fear; overpowering fear. See fright and terror.

parry—A defensive technique: a quick, forceful slap that redirects an assailant's linear attack. There are two types of parries: horizontal and vertical.

passive response—One of the three possible counters when assaulted by a grab, choke, or hold from a standing position. Passive response requires you to nullify the assault without injuring your adversary. See aggressive response and moderate response.

patience—A combative attribute. The ability to endure and tolerate difficulty.

perception—Interpretation of vital information acquired from your senses when faced with a potentially threatening situation.

philosophical resolution—The act of analyzing and answering various questions concerning the use of violence in defense of yourself and others.

philosophy—One of the five aspects of CFA's mental component. A deep state of introspection whereby you methodically resolve critical questions concerning the use of force in defense of yourself or others.

physical attributes—The numerous physical qualities that enhance your combative skills and abilities.

physical component—One of the three vital components of the CFA system. The physical component includes the physical aspects of fighting, such as physical fitness, weapon/technique mastery, and combative attributes. See mental component and spiritual component.

physical conditioning—See combative fitness.

physical fitness—See combative fitness.

positional asphyxia—The arrangement, placement, or positioning of your opponent's body in such a way as to interrupt your breathing and cause unconsciousness or possibly death.

positioning—The spatial relationship of the assailant to the assailed person in terms of target exposure, escape, angle of attack, and various other strategic considerations.

postal attack - see going postal.

power—A physical attribute of armed and unarmed combat. The amount of force you can generate when striking an anatomical target.

power generators—Specific points on your body that generate impact power. There are three anatomical power generators: shoulders, hips, and feet.

precision—See accuracy.

preemptive strike—See first strike.

premise—An axiom, concept, rule, or any other valid reason to modify or go beyond that which has been established.

preparedness—A state of being ready for combat. There are three components of preparedness: affective preparedness, cognitive preparedness, and psychomotor preparedness.

probable reaction dynamics - The opponent's anticipated or predicted movements or actions during both armed and unarmed combat.

proficiency training—A CFA training methodology requiring the practitioner to execute a specific body weapon, technique, maneuver, or tactic over and over for a prescribed number of repetitions. See conditioning training and street training.

progressive indirect attack (PIA) – One of the five methods of attack. A progressive method of attack whereby the initial tool or technique is designed to set the opponent up for follow-up blows.

proxemics—The study of the nature and effect of man's personal space.

proximity—The ability to maintain a strategically safe distance from a threatening individual.

pseudospeciation—A combative attribute. The tendency to assign subhuman and inferior qualities to a threatening assailant.

psychological conditioning—The process of conditioning the mind for the horrors and rigors of real combat.

psychomotor preparedness—One of the three components of preparedness. Psychomotor preparedness means possessing all of the physical skills and attributes necessary to defeat a formidable adversary. See affective preparedness and cognitive preparedness.

punch—A quick, forceful strike of the fists.

punching range—One of the three ranges of unarmed combat. Punching range is the mid range of unarmed combat from which the fighter uses his hands to strike his assailant. See kicking range and grappling range.

punching-range tools—The various body weapons that are employed in the punching range of unarmed combat, including finger jabs, palm-heel strikes, rear cross, knife-hand strikes, horizontal and shovel hooks, uppercuts, and hammer-fist strikes. See grappling-range tools and kicking-range tools.

Q

qualities of combat—See attributes of combat.

quarter beat - One of the four beat classifications of the Widow Maker Program. Quarter beat strikes never break contact with the assailant's face. Quarter beat strikes are primarily responsible for creating the psychological panic and trauma when Razing.

R

range—The spatial relationship between a fighter and a threatening assailant.

range deficiency—The inability to effectively fight and defend in all ranges of combat (armed and unarmed).

range manipulation—A combative attribute. The strategic manipulation of combat ranges.

range proficiency—A combative attribute. The ability to effectively fight and defend in all ranges of combat (armed and unarmed).

ranges of engagement—See combat ranges.

ranges of unarmed combat—The three distances (kicking range, punching range, and grappling range) a fighter might physically engage with an assailant while involved in unarmed combat.

raze – To level, demolish or obliterate.

razer – One who performs the Razing methodology.

razing – The second phase of the Widow Maker Program. A series of vicious close quarter techniques designed to physically and psychologically extirpate a criminal attacker.

razing amplifier - a technique, tactic or procedure that magnifies the destructiveness of your razing technique.

reaction dynamics—see probable reaction dynamics.

reaction time—The elapsed time between a stimulus and the response to that particular stimulus. See offensive reaction time and defensive reaction time.

rear cross—A straight punch delivered from the rear hand that crosses from right to left (if in a left stance) or left to right (if in a right stance).

rear side—The side of the body furthest from the assailant. See lead side.

reasonable force—That degree of force which is not excessive for a particular event and which is appropriate in protecting yourself or others.

refinement—The strategic and methodical process of improving or perfecting.

relocation principle—Also known as relocating, this is a street-fighting tactic that requires you to immediately move to a new location (usually by flanking your adversary) after delivering a compound attack.

repetition—Performing a single movement, exercise, strike, or action continuously for a specific period.

research—A scientific investigation or inquiry.

rhythm—Movements characterized by the natural ebb and flow of related elements.

ritual-oriented training—Formalized training that is conducted without intrinsic purpose. See combat-oriented training and sport-oriented training.

S

safety—One of the three criteria for a CFA body weapon, technique, maneuver, or tactic. It means that the tool, technique, maneuver or tactic provides the least amount of danger and risk for the practitioner. See efficiency and effectiveness.

scissors hold—See guard position.

scorching – Quickly and inconspicuously applying oleoresin capsicum (hot pepper extract) on your fingertips and then razing your adversary.

self-awareness—One of the three categories of CFA awareness. Knowing and understanding yourself. This includes aspects of yourself which may provoke criminal violence and which will promote a proper and strong reaction to an attack. See criminal awareness and situational awareness.

self-confidence—Having trust and faith in yourself.

self-enlightenment—The state of knowing your capabilities, limitations, character traits, feelings, general attributes, and motivations. See self-awareness.

set—A term used to describe a grouping of repetitions.

shadow fighting—A CFA training exercise used to develop and refine your tools, techniques, and attributes of armed and unarmed combat.

sharking – A counter attack technique that is used when your adversary grabs your razing hand.

shielding wedge - a defensive maneuver used to counter an unarmed postal attack.

simple direct attack (SDA) – One of the five methods of attack. A method of attack whereby the practitioner delivers a solitary offense tool or technique. It may involve a series of discrete probes or one swift, powerful strike aimed at terminating the encounter.

situational awareness—One of the three categories of CFA awareness. A state of being totally alert to your immediate surroundings, including people, places, objects, and actions. (See criminal awareness and self-awareness.)

skeletal alignment—The proper alignment or arrangement of your body. Skeletal alignment maximizes the structural integrity of striking tools.

skills—One of the three factors that determine who will win a street fight. Skills refers to psychomotor proficiency with the tools and techniques of combat. See Attitude and Knowledge.

slipping—A defensive maneuver that permits you to avoid an assailant's linear blow without stepping out of range. Slipping can be accomplished by quickly snapping the head and upper torso sideways (right or left) to avoid the blow.

snap back—A defensive maneuver that permits you to avoid an assailant's linear and circular blows without stepping out of range. The snap back can be accomplished by quickly snapping the head backward to avoid the assailant's blow.

somatotypes—A method of classifying human body types or builds into three different categories: endomorph, mesomorph, and ectomorph. See endomorph, mesomorph, and ectomorph.

sparring—A training exercise where two or more fighters fight each other while wearing protective equipment.

speed—A physical attribute of armed and unarmed combat. The rate or a measure of the rapid rate of motion.

spiritual component—One of the three vital components of the CFA system. The spiritual component includes the metaphysical issues and aspects of existence. See physical component and mental component.

sport-oriented training—Training that is geared for competition and governed by a set of rules. See combat-oriented training and ritual-oriented training.

sprawling—A grappling technique used to counter a double- or single-leg takedown.

square off—To be face-to-face with a hostile or threatening assailant who is about to attack you.

stance—One of the many strategic postures you assume prior to or during armed or unarmed combat.

stick fighting—Fighting that takes place with either one or two sticks.

strategic positioning—Tactically positioning yourself to either escape, move behind a barrier, or use a makeshift weapon.

strategic/tactical development—One of the five elements of CFA's mental component.

strategy—A carefully planned method of achieving your goal of engaging an assailant under advantageous conditions.

street fight—A spontaneous and violent confrontation between two or more individuals wherein no rules apply.

street fighter—An unorthodox combatant who has no formal training. His combative skills and tactics are usually developed in the street by the process of trial and error.

street training—A CFA training methodology requiring the practitioner to deliver explosive compound attacks for 10 to 20 seconds. See condition ng training and proficiency training.

strength training—The process of developing muscular strength through systematic application of progressive resistance.

striking art—A combat art that relies predominantly on striking techniques to neutralize or terminate a criminal attacker.

striking shield—A rectangular shield constructed of foam and vinyl used to develop power in your kicks, punches, and strikes.

striking tool—A natural body weapon that impacts with the assailant's anatomical target.

strong side—The strongest and most coordinated side of your body.

structure—A definite and organized pattern.

style—The distinct manner in which a fighter executes or performs his combat skills.

stylistic integration—The purposeful and scientific collection of tools and techniques from various disciplines, which are strategically integrated and dramatically altered to meet three essential criteria: efficiency, effectiveness, and combative safety.

submission holds—Also known as control and restraint techniques, many of these locks and holds create sufficient pain to cause the adversary to submit.

system—The unification of principles, philosophies, rules, strategies, methodologies, tools, and techniques of a particular method of combat.

T

tactic—The skill of using the available means to achieve an end.

target awareness—A combative attribute that encompasses five strategic principles: target orientation, target recognition, target selection, target impaction, and target exploitation.

target exploitation—A combative attribute. The strategic maximization of your assailant's reaction dynamics during a fight. Target exploitation can be applied in both armed and unarmed encounters.

target impaction—The successful striking of the appropriate anatomical target.

target orientation—A combative attribute. Having a workable knowledge of the assailant's anatomical targets.

target recognition—The ability to immediately recognize appropriate anatomical targets during an emergency self-defense situation.

target selection—The process of mentally selecting the appropriate anatomical target for your self-defense situation. This is predicated on certain factors, including proper force response, assailant's positioning, and range.

target stare—A form of telegraphing in which you stare at the anatomical target you intend to strike.

target zones—The three areas in which an assailant's anatomical targets are located. (See zone one, zone two and zone three.)

technique—A systematic procedure by which a task is accomplished.

telegraphic cognizance—A combative attribute. The ability to recognize both verbal and non-verbal signs of aggression or assault.

telegraphing—Unintentionally making your intentions known to your adversary.

tempo—The speed or rate at which you speak.

terminate—To kill.

terror—The third stage of fear; defined as overpowering fear. See fright and panic.

timing—A physical and mental attribute of armed and unarmed combat. Your ability to execute a movement at the optimum moment.

tone—The overall quality or character of your voice.

tool—See body weapon.

traditional martial arts—Any martial art that fails to evolve and change to meet the demands and characteristics of its present environment.

traditional style/system—See traditional martial arts.

training drills—The various exercises and drills aimed at perfecting combat skills, attributes, and tactics.

trap and tuck – A counter move technique used when the adversary attempts to raze you during your quarter beat assault.

U

unified mind—A mind free and clear of distractions and focused on the combative situation.

use of force response—A combative attribute. Selecting the appropriate level of force for a particular emergency self-defense situation.

V

viciousness—A combative attribute. The propensity to be extremely violent and destructive often characterized by intense savagery.

violence—The intentional utilization of physical force to coerce, injure, cripple, or kill.

visualization—Also known as mental visualization or mental imagery. The purposeful formation of mental images and scenarios in the mind's eye.

W

warm-up—A series of mild exercises, stretches, and movements designed to prepare you for more intense exercise.

weak side—The weaker and more uncoordinated side of your body.

weapon and technique mastery—A component of CFA's physical component. The kinesthetic and psychomotor development of a weapon or combative technique.

weapon capability—An assailant's ability to use and attack with a particular weapon.

webbing - The first phase of the Widow Maker Program. Webbing is a two hand strike delivered to the assailant's chin. It is called Webbing because your hands resemble a large web that wraps around the enemy's face.

widow maker – One who makes widows by destroying husbands.

widow maker program – A CFA combat program specifically designed to teach the law abiding citizen how to use extreme force when faced with immediate threat of unlawful deadly criminal attack. The Widow Maker program is divided into two phases or methodologies: Webbing and Razing.

Y

yell—A loud and aggressive scream or shout used for various strategic reasons.

Z

zero beat – One of the four beat classifications of the Widow Maker, Feral Fighting and Savage Street Fighting Programs. Zero beat strikes are full pressure techniques applied to a specific target until it completely ruptures. They include gouging, crushing, biting, and choking techniques.

zone one—Anatomical targets related to your senses, including the eyes, temple, nose, chin, and back of neck.

zone three—Anatomical targets related to your mobility, including thighs, knees, shins, and instep.

zone two—Anatomical targets related to your breathing, including front of neck, solar plexus, ribs, and groin.

Knife Fighting Targets

About Sammy Franco

With over 35 years of experience, Sammy Franco is one of the world's foremost authorities on armed and unarmed self-defense. Highly regarded as a leading innovator in combat sciences, Mr. Franco was one of the premier pioneers in the field of "reality-based" self-defense and martial arts instruction.

Sammy Franco is perhaps best known as the founder and creator of Contemporary Fighting Arts (CFA), a state-of-the-art offensive-based combat system that is specifically designed for real-world self-defense. CFA is a sophisticated and practical system of self-defense, designed specifically to provide efficient and effective methods to avoid, defuse, confront, and neutralize both armed and unarmed attackers.

Sammy Franco has frequently been featured in martial art magazines, newspapers, and appeared on numerous radio and television programs. Mr. Franco has also authored numerous books, magazine articles, and editorials, and has developed a popular library of instructional videos.

Sammy Franco's experience and credibility in the combat sciences is unequaled. One of his many accomplishments in this field includes the fact that he has earned the ranking of a Law Enforcement Master Instructor, and has designed, implemented, and taught officer survival training to the United States Border Patrol (USBP). He has instructed members of the US Secret Service, Military Special Forces, Washington DC Police Department, Montgomery County, Maryland

Deputy Sheriffs, and the US Library of Congress Police. Sammy Franco is also a member of the prestigious International Law Enforcement Educators and Trainers Association (ILEETA) as well as the American Society of Law Enforcement Trainers (ASLET) and he is listed in the "Who's Who Director of Law Enforcement Instructors."

Sammy Franco is a nationally certified Law Enforcement Instructor in the following curricula: PR-24 Side-Handle Baton, Police Arrest and Control Procedures, Police Personal Weapons Tactics, Police Power Handcuffing Methods, Police Oleoresin Capsicum Aerosol Training (OCAT), Police Weapon Retention and Disarming Methods, Police Edged Weapon Countermeasures and "Use of Force" Assessment and Response Methods.

Mr. Franco holds a Bachelor of Arts degree in Criminal Justice from the University of Maryland. He is a regularly featured speaker at a number of professional conferences and conducts dynamic and enlightening seminars on numerous aspects of self-defense and combat training.

On a personal level, Sammy Franco is an animal lover, who will go to great lengths to assist and rescue animals. Throughout the years, he's rescued everything from turkey vultures to goats. However, his most treasured moments are always spent with his beloved German Shepherd dogs.

For more information about Mr. Franco and his unique Contemporary Fighting Arts system, you can visit his website at: **ContemporaryFightingArts.com** or follow him on twitter @ **RealSammyFranco**

Other Books by Sammy Franco

SURVIVAL WEAPONS
A User's Guide to the Best Self-Defense Weapons for Surviving Any Dangerous Situation
by Sammy Franco

Whether you are just commuting around town or preparing for a SHTF scenario, Survival Weapons: A User's Guide to the Best Self-Defense Weapons for Surviving Any Dangerous Situation teaches you how to choose with the most efficient weapons for any survival situation. A must-have book for anyone interested in real world survival and wants to dramatically improve their odds of prevailing in any high-risk combat situation. 8.5 x 5.5, paperback, photos, illus, 210 pages.

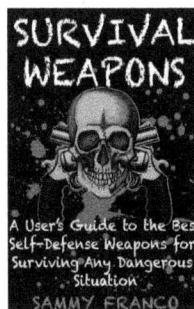

CANE FIGHTING
The Authoritative Guide to Using the Cane or Walking Stick for Self-Defense
by Sammy Franco

Cane Fighting: The Authoritative Guide to Using the Cane or Walking Stick for Self-Defense is a no nonsense book written for anyone who wants to learn how to use the cane or walking stick as a fighting weapon for real-world self-defense. With over 200 photographs and step-by-step instructions, Cane Fighting is the authoritative resource for mastering the Hooked Wooden Cane, Modern Tactical Combat Cane, Walking Sticks, Irish Fighting Shillelagh and the Bo Staff: 8.5 x 5.5, paperback, photos, illus, 242 pages.

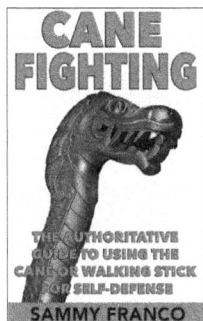

KNOCKOUT
The Ultimate Guide to Sucker Punching
by Sammy Franco

Knockout is a one-of-a-kind book designed to teach you the lost art and science of sucker punching for real-world self-defense situations. With over 150 detailed photographs, 244 pages and dozens of easy-to-follow instructions, Knockout has everything you need to master the devastating art of sucker punching. Whether you are a beginner or advanced, student or teacher, Knockout teaches you brutally effective skills, battle-tested techniques, and proven strategies to get you home alive and in one piece. 8.5 x 5.5, paperback, 244 pages.

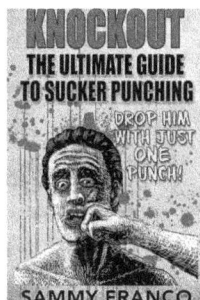

SAVAGE STREET FIGHTING
Tactical Savagery as a Last Resort
by Sammy Franco

In this revolutionary book, Sammy Franco reveals the science behind his most primal street fighting method. Savage Street Fighting is a brutal self-defense system specifically designed to teach the law-abiding citizen how to use "Tactical Savagery" when faced with the immediate threat of an unlawful deadly criminal attack. Savage Street Fighting is systematically engineered to protect you when there are no other self-defense options left! With over 300 photographs and detailed step-by-step instructions, Savage Street Fighting is a must-have book for anyone concerned about real world self-defense. Now is the time to learn how to unleash your inner beast! 8.5 x 5.5, paperback, 317 photos, illustrations, 232 pages.

FIRST STRIKE
End a Fight in Ten Seconds or Less!
by Sammy Franco

Learn how to stop any attack before it starts by mastering the art of the preemptive strike. First Strike gives you an easy-to-learn yet highly effective self-defense game plan for handling violent close-quarter combat encounters. First Strike will teach you instinctive, practical and realistic self-defense techniques that will drop any criminal attacker to the floor with one punishing blow. By reading this book and by practicing, you will learn the hard-hitting skills necessary to execute a punishing first strike and ultimately prevail in a self-defense situation. And that's what it is all about: winning in as little time as possible. 8.5 x 5.5, paperback, photos, illustrations, 202 pages.

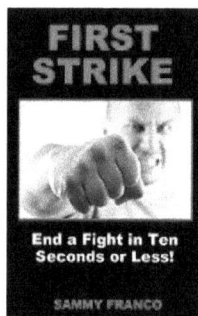

WAR MACHINE
How to Transform Yourself Into A Vicious & Deadly Street Fighter
by Sammy Franco

War Machine is a book that will change you for the rest of your life! When followed accordingly, War Machine will forge your mind, body and spirit into iron. Once armed with the mental and physical attributes of the War Machine, you will become a strong and confident warrior that can handle just about anything that life may throw your way. In essence, War Machine is a way of life. Powerful, intense, and hard. 11 x 8.5, paperback, photos, illustrations, 210 pages.